# Easy Spanish Phrase Book

*The 2000 Most Common Phrases for Travel & Everyday Life*

FLUENCY FASTER

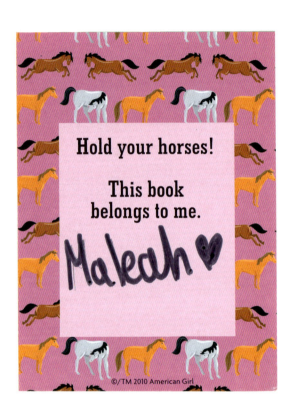

Hold your horses!

This book
belongs to me.

Maleah ♥

# Contents

# Claim Your FREE Bonus!

## **LIMITED OFFER**

We are giving away our **best-selling** Spanish Short Stories book to the first 200 customers!

All you have to do is scan QR code with your phone camera below and follow the instructions to get your **FREE** free copy of:

**"Spanish Short Stories: 25 Engaging Short Stories to Build Your Vocabulary and Learn the Fast & Fun Way!"**

**Valued at $15.99!**

Hurry, once **200 readers** have scanned the QR code this offer will expire!

# Introduction

Whether you are planning your next trip, trying to jump start your Spanish lessons, or simply need a quick reference when speaking to your Latin American neighbor - you've picked the perfect companion phrasebook.

Not only will this book teach you all of the most common Spanish phrases that are actually used by natives, but will also assist you in navigating the slew of different situations you may find yourself in: From arriving at the airport, getting around, town meeting new friends, being courteous, and even dreaded life and death emergencies – a scary thought but a stark reality that you should always be prepared for.

We have focused on the most useful phrases and omitted the random filler phrases that you will so often find in other "best selling" phrasebooks – phrases that, quite frankly, you will never EVER use.

Aside from the traveling tourist, this book is also a fantastic resource for those who have a large Spanish speaking population living their home country. Keep it in your car, throw it in your backpack or handbag – you really never know when you may need it.

Get ready to feel confident in any situation and never be embarrassed by those awkward silences and judgmental looks. You'll never be seen as "just another gringo" again!

# How to use this book effectively

This book chapters have been organized according to common scenarios of daily life, which make searching for the most fitting phrase quick and easy. Whatever situation you find yourself in, simply flip to the correct chapter and choose the from the list of relevant phrases. In the first column you will find the English phrase, the second is the Spanish translation and just underneath the translation you will find the simple phonetic pronunciation guide.

We have also arranged the chapters intelligently with the most frequently used phrases at the start of the book are ones that are used less more toward the end. This makes it easy for you find that perfect phrase quicker than ever!

In the chapter of the book we'll start off with proper pronunciation, keeping it simple and practical without getting too technical.

We hope you enjoy using this book as much as we have enjoyed creating it for you!

*Gracias!*

# Phonetic Pronunciation

This section contains the phonetic transcription of the Spanish alphabet, which is essential to learn the correct pronunciation of the words. Even though the Spanish sound scheme can seem highly different from the English one, with time and practice you shall get used to the Spanish sounds and the phonetic transcriptions of the words.

In order to facilitate the process of learning, the transcriptions provided in this book follow the rules of English spelling and pronunciation. For instance, the consonant "g" changes its pronunciation depending on the vowel that goes with it. If "g" goes with "a", it sounds as in "garden" but, if it goes with "e", it sounds as in "general"; ect. The syllables that have to be stressed will be written in capital letters.

This book provides a "neutral" Spanish dialect and pronunciation that should be understood by any Spanish-speaking country.

## Phonetic transcription:

| | |
|---|---|
| ah | short A as in **abide or a**lphabet |
| ay | long A as in w**ait, ei**ght or d**ay**time |
| ch | as in **ch**apter or resear**ch** |
| eh | short E as in **e**lephant or cinema |
| ee | long E as in singl**e** or gr**ee**n |
| g | as in **g**et, **g**oal or alle**g**ation |
| h | as in **h**eel or **h**andful |
| k | hard C as in **c**ow, dedi**c**ation or s**c**reen |

| | |
|---|---|
| ny | as in u**ny**oke |
| oh | short O as in **o**bsession or p**oi**nt |
| oo | long O as in n**oo**dle or l**oo**se |
| s | as in **s**un or univer**s**ity |
| w | as in **w**ood or **w**itness |
| y | as in **y**esterday or **y**aw |

# Spanish Pronunciation

## Vowels

Spanish vowels can be either strong or weak. Strong vowels are pronounced with an open mouth and they are **a-e-o**. On the other hand, weak vowels do not require opening the mouth and these are **i-u**. The pronunciation of Spanish vowels is usually shorter than the English vowels.

### Vowel A

The Spanish sound for **a** is similar to the "a" in alphabet. The reader should pronounce it always in this way.

| | |
|---|---|
| Amigo (friend) | Abuela (grandmother) |
| Ansiedad (anxiety) | Había (there was) |

In the case that the vowel is written with an accent, it has to be pronounced with more emphasis in that syllable when the reader speaks.

### Vowel E

The Spanish pronunciation for **e** sounds like the first "e" in "elections". The reader will always use the same pronunciation for this vowel.

| | |
|---|---|
| Esperar (to wait) | Elegante (elegant) |
| Teatro (theatre) | Enemigo (enemy) |

The vowel **i** sounds like the double "e" in English. It is similar to the pronunciation of "leaf" or "wheel", but shorter.

Idioma (language)

Isla (island)

This vowel has the same sound as "o" in orange.

Operación (operation)

Oro (gold)

The sound for **u** in Spanish is equivalent to the sound of double "o". However, the pronunciation in Spanish needs to be shorter.

Universo (universe)

Uso (use)

Also, in Spanish we can find vowel combinations such as AE, UI, EO... The reader needs to remember to pronounce all vowels respectively. There are some examples below:

| AE | UI |
|---|---|
| ah eh - Aeronáutica | oo ee - Cuidar |

# Consonants

Most of the consonants have the same pronunciation in English than in Spanish. However, in some cases, their pronunciation can be altered. In this section, we are going to show the reader the more significant consonants.

## Consonant C + a-e-o

The pronunciation of consonant c will vary depending on the vowels next to it. If the consonant is followed by the vowels a-e-o, it sounds like "k".

Cosa (thing)                    Camello (camel)

koh-sah                         Kah-meh-yoh

Cuerda (rope)

Koo-ehr-dah

## Consonant C + i-e

When c is followed by the vowels i-e, the pronunciation changes and it is pronounced as "s".

Cisne (swan)

Sees-neh

Cómplice (accomplice)

kohm-plee-she

## Consonant C+H

This consonant is formed by the combination of two different ones. Generally, the pronunciation is similar to "ch" in English words like "cheese" or "change".

Chica (girl)

chee-kah

## Consonant G+a-o-u

The pronunciation of g also changes depending on the vowel next to it. When it goes with a-o-u, g is pronounced as in "goal".

Gamba (prawn)

gahm-bah

Gusto (taste)

goohs-to

## Consonant G + e-i

When g goes with e or i, it sounds like the Spanish consonant "j". The pronunciation resembles the English pronunciation of "h" in "hunt".

Gemelos (twins)

heh-meh-lohs

Sometimes, we can find the consonant g with "ui" or "ue". In that case, the sound will be as the "g" in "goal".

Ceguera (blindness)

seh-geh-rah

## Consonant H

In Spanish, the consonant h at the beginning of a word does not have a sound. It is always silent.

Historia (history)

ees-toh-ree-ah

Hueso (bone)

oo-eh-soh

## Consonant LL

The Spanish pronunciation for double L is equivalent to the English pronunciation of "y" in "yesterday" or "j" in "june".

Lluvia (rain)

yoo-vee-ah

llegar (to arrive)

yeh-gahr

## Consonant Ñ

This consonant can be found on

in the Spanish alphabet. The pronunciation is similar to the sound "ny" in English.

Enseñar (to teach)

ehn-seh-nyahr

Año (year)

ah-nyoh

## Consonant P

This consonant will always sound as the "p" in "paper". It is never aspirated.

Piedra (rock)

pee-eh-drah

aspirar (inhale)

ahs-pee-rahr

## Consonant Q

The pronunciation of this consonant is just like the sound "k". We will always find it followed by "ue" or "ui" as in "queue".

Quedar (to meet)

keh-dahr

## Consonant R

The consonant R can be double or single. When it is double, the pronunciation is strong and requires the vibration of the tongue in the palate.

Regalo (gift)

reh-gah-loh

When we have a soft "r", the pronunciation is similar to a faint "r". This resembles the "r" in the word "running".

Cara (face)

kah-rah

Esperar (to wait)

ehs-peh-rahr

## Consonant T

This consonant always sounds as the "t" in "terrace"

# Greetings

Hello
*Hola*
OH-lah

Good morning
*Buenos días*
BWEH-nohs DEE-ahs

Good afternoon
*Buenas tardes*
BWEN-nahs TAHR-dehs

Good evening
*Buenas noches*
BWEH-nahs NOH-chehs

Hi
*Buenas*
BWEH-nahs

Whats up?
*¿Qué pasa?*
KEH PAH-sah

What is your name?
*¿Cómo te llamas?*
KOH-moh teh YAH-mahs

It's a pleasure to see you again
*Un placer volver a verte*
oon plah-SEHR bohl-BEHR ah BEHR-teh

It's good to see you
*Qué bueno verte*
Keh BWEH-noh BEHR-teh

How are you?
*¿Qué tal?*
KEH tahl

How's it going?
*¿Cómo te va*
KOH-moh teh bah

How was your day?
*¿Qué tal tu día?*
KEH tahl too DEE-ah?

How is your night going?
*¿Cómo va tu noche?*
KOH-moh bah too NOH-cheh

What's happening?
*¿Qué está pasando?*
Keh ehs-TAH pah-SAHN-doh

It's been a long time
*Ha pasado mucho tiempo*
Ah pah-SAH-doh MOO-choh Tee-EHM-poh

How is everything?
*¿Qué tal todo?*
KEH tahl TOH-doh

Let me introduce you to..
*Déjame presentarte a…*
DEH-ha-meh preh-sehn-TAHR-teh ah

Good day to you
*Que tengas un buen día*
Keh TEHN-gahs oon boo-EHN DEE-ah

15

**What are you up to?**
*¿Qué estás haciendo?*
Keh ehs-TAHS ah-cee-EHN-doh

**Where have you been hiding?**
¿Dónde has estado escondido?
DOHN-deh ahs ehs-TAH-doh ehs-kohn-DEE-doh

**When are you coming?**
*¿Cuándo vienes?*
KWAHN-doh vee-EH-nehs

**I've been looking for you**
*Te he estado buscando*
Teh eh ehs-TAH-doh boos-KAHN-doh

**Welcome**
*Bienvenido*
Bee-ehn-beh-NEE-doh

**Come in**
*Adelante*
ah-deh-LAHN-teh

**I hope you are having a great day**
*Espero que tengas un gran día*
Ehs-PEH-roh keh TEHN-gahs oon grahn DEE-ah

**Long time no see**
*Cuánto tiempo sin verte*
KWAHN-toh tee-EHM-poh seen BEHR-teh

**Take care**
*Cuidate*
Koo-EE-dah-teh

**Do you know…?**
*¿Conoces a …?*
Koh-NOH-sehs ah

**Let me introduce myself.**
**My name is -**
*Permítame presentarme. Mi nombre es -*
pehr-MEE-tah-meh preh-sehn-TAHR-meh. Meh YAH-moh

## Responses

**My name is…**
*Me nombre es…*
Mee – nom – breh – esh

**It's a pleasure to meet you**
*Es un placer conocerte*
Ehs oon plah-SEHR koh-noh-SEHR-teh

**Nice to meet you**
*Encantado de conocerte*
Ehn-kahn-TAH -do deh koh-noh-SEHR-teh

**Good thanks, and you?**
*Bien, gracias. ¿ Y tú?*
Bee- EHN GRAH-seeahs ee too

**You're welcome**
*De nada*
Deh NAH-dah

**Come in**
*Pasa / Adelante*
PAH-sah / Ah-deh-lahn-teh

**I am having a good day**
*Estoy teniendo un buen día*
Ehs-TOH-ee teh-nee-EHN-doh oon boo-EHN DEE-ah

**It's been too long**
*Ha pasado mucho tiempo*
Ah pah-SAH-doh MOO-choh tee-EHM-poh

**I'm good, and you?**
*Estoy bien, ¿ Y tú?*
ehs-TOH-ee bee-EHN – ee TOO

**I don't feel well**
*No me siento bien*
Noh meh see-EHN-toh bee-EHN

**I am tired**
*Estoy cansado* Ehs-TOH-ee kahn-SAH-doh

**Yes, I know...**
*Si, conozco a...*
Seeh koh-NOHS-koh ah

**I am so-so**
*Estoy regular*
Ehs-TOH-ee reh-goo-LAHR

**Yes, I had a good time.**
*Sí, lo pasé bien*
See, loh pah-SEH bee-EHN

# Common Courtesy

**Thank you**
*Gracias*
GRAH-seeahs

**Thank you very much**
*Muchas gracias*
MOO-chahs GRAH-see-ahs

**A thousand thank yous**
*Mil gracias*
meel GRAH-see-ahs

**Thank you for your help**
*Gracias por tu ayuda*
GRAH-see-ahs pohr too a-YOO-dah

**No, thank you**
*No, gracias*
*Noh* GRAH-see-ahs

**Please**
*Por favor*
Pohr fah-VOHR

**May I?**
*¿Me permite?*
Meh pehr-MEE-teh

Excuse me / Pardon me
*Disculpe / perdóneme*
Dees-KOOL-peh/ pehr-DOH-neh-me

**Yes please**
*Sí, por favor.*
See pohr fah-VOHR

**You speak English very well**
*Hablas inglés muy bien.*
AH-blahs een-GLEHS MOO-ee bee-EHN

**I don't speak Spanish very well**
*No hablo muy bien español*
Noh AH-bloh MOO-ch bee-EHN ehs-pah-NYOHL

**This is my first time in your lovely country**
*Esta es mi primera vez en tu hermoso país*
EHS-tah ehs mee pree-MEH-rah vehs chn too ehr-MOH-soh pah-EES

**Your country is very beautiful**
*Tu país es muy bello*
Too pah-EES ehs MOO-ee BEH-yoh

17

**You look great!**
*¡Te ves genial!*
Teh vehs heh-nee-AHL

**Wait a moment, please**
*Espera un momento, por favor*
Ehs-PEH-rah oon moh-MEHN-toh pohr
fah-VOHR

**With your permission**
*Con tu permiso*
Kohn too pehr-MEE-soh

**If there is anything you want, tell me**
*Si quieres algo, dímelo*
See kee-EH-rehs AHL-goh DEE-meh-loh

**Please take care of yourself**
*Por favor, cuídate*
Pohr fah-VOHR koo-EE-dah-teh

**I don't want to bother you anymore, so I will go**
*No quiero molestarte más, así que me iré*
Noh kee-EH-roh moh-lehs-TAHR-teh
mahs ah-SEE keh meh ee-REH

**What can I help you with?**
*¿En qué te puedo ayudar?*
En keh teh poo-EH-doh ah-yoo-DAHR

**I can help you with that**
*Te puedo ayudar con eso*
Teh poo-EH-doh a-YOOH-dahr kohn
EH-soh

**You don't have manners**
*No tienes educación*
Noh tee-EH-nehs eh-doo-kah-see-OHN

**You're welcome**
*De nada*
Deh NAH-dah

**No problem**
*No hay problema*
Noh AH-ee proh-BLEH-mah

**My pleasure / It's a pleasure / With pleasure**
*El gusto es mío / Un placer / Con gusto*
Ehl GOOS-toh ehs MEE-oh / Oon plah-SEHR / Kohn GOOS-toh

**The pleasure is mine**
*El placer es mío*
Ehl plah-SEHR ehs MEE-oh

**Yes, you may**
*Sí, puedes*
Seeh, poo-EH-dehs

**No, I don't need your help**
*No, no necesito tu ayuda*
Noh noh neh-seh-SEE-toh too ah-YOO-dah

**You are very well educated**
*Estás muy bien educado*
Ehs-TAHS MOO-ee bee-EHN eh-doo-KAH-doh

**Make yourself at home**
*Esta es tu casa*
EHS-tah ehs too KAH-sah

18

# Farewells

See you later
*Te veo después*
Teh VEH-oh dehs-poo-EHS

See ya
*Nos vemos*
Nohs VEH-mohs

**Goodbye**
*Adiós*
Ah-dee-OHS

Later
*Después*
Dehs-poo-EHS

**Take care**
*Cuídate*
Koo-EH-dah-teh

Have a nice day
*Que tengas un buen día*
Keh TEHN-gahs oon boo-EHN DEE-ah

See you soon
*Nos vemos pronto*
Nohs VEH-mohs PROHN-toh

**Until we see each other again**
*Hasta la próxima*
AHS-tah la PRO ksee mah

**We'll see each other**
*Nos veremos*
Nohs veh-REH-mohs

**It was nice to see you**
*Fue agradable verte*
Foo-EH ah-grah-DAH-bleh VEHR-teh

See you tomorrow
*Nos vemos mañana*
Nohs VEH-mohs ma-NYAH-nah

See you next week
*Nos vemos la semana que viene*
Nohs VEH-mohs lah seh-MAH-nah keh vee-EH-neh

**Talk to you later**
*Hablamos después*
Ah-BLAH-mohs dehs-poo-EHS

**I will come back tomorrow**
*Volveré mañana*
Vohl-veh-REH mah-NYAH-nah

**I have got to get going**
*Tengo que irme*
TEHN-goh keh EER-meh

**See you when you get back**
*Nos vemos a la vuelta*
Nohs VEH-mohs ah lah voo-EHL-tah

**We will see each other again in a different life**
*Nos volveremos a ver en otra vida*
Nohs vohl-veh-REH-mohs ah vehr ehn OH-trah VEE-dah

19

# Giving your opinion

**What do you think about it?**
*¿Qué piensas de esto?*
Keh pee-EHN-sahs deh EHS-toh

**Tell me what you think**
*Dime que piensas*
DEE-meh keh pee-EHN-sahs

**Do you have a different opinion?**
*¿Tienes una opinión diferente?*
Tee-EH-nehs OO-nah oh-pee-nee-OHN
dee-feh-REHN-teh

**Honestly, I don't think we should say that**
*Sinceramente, no pienso que debamos decir eso*
Seen-seh-rah-MEHN-teh noh pee-EHN-soh keh deh-BAH-mohs deh-SEER EH-soh

**Your words are meaningless to me**
*Tus palabras no significan nada para mi*
Toos pah-LAH-brahs noh seeg-nee-FEE-kahn NAH-dah PAH-rah mee

**This is my opinion**
*Esta es mi opinión*
EHS-tah ehs mee oh-pee-nee-OHN

**I don't think so**
*No pienso eso*
Noh pee-EHN-soh EH-soh

**Why do you think that?**
*¿Por qué piensas eso?*
pohr KEH pee-EHN-sahs EH-soh

**Sorry to interrupt**
*Lamento interrumpir*
Lah-MEHN-toh een-teh-rrohm-PEER

**I really think that…**
*Realmente pienso que…*
reh-ahl-MEHN-teh pee-EHN-soh keh

**You are right**
*Tienes razon*
Tee-EH-nehs rah-SOHN

**I agree with you**
*Estoy de acuerdo contigo*
Ehs-TOH-eh deh ah-koo-EHR-doh kohn-TEE-goh

**I disagree with my friends in this topic**
*No estoy de acuerdo con mis amigos en este tema*
Noh ehs-TOH-ee deh ah-koo-EHR-doh kohn mees ah-MEE-gohs ehn EHS-teh TEH-mah

**That is not always the same**
*Eso no es siempre igual*
EH-soh noh ehs see-EHM-preh ee-goo AHL

## Not everyone has to have the same opinion than you
*No todo el mundo tiene que tener la misma opinión que tú*
Noh TOH-doh ehl MOON-doh tee-EH-neh keh teh-NEHR lah MEES-mah oh-pee-nee-OHN keh too

## We don't need to argue over this
*No necesitamos discutir por esto*
Noh neh-seh-see-TAH-mohs dees-koo-TEER por EHS-toh

## You are allowed to have your own opinion
*Puedes tener tu propia opinión*
PWEH-dehs teh-NEHR too PROH-pee-ah oh-pee-nee-OHN

## Is your argument justified?
*¿Tu argumento tiene justificación?*
Too ahr-goo-MEHN-toh tee-EH-neh hoos-tee-fee-kah-see-OHN

## Yes, I accept your way of thinking
*Sí, acepto tu modo de pensar*
See, ah-SEHP-toh too MOH-doh deh pehn-SAHR

## From my point of view, what you are saying is wrong
*Desde mi punto de vista, lo que estás diciendo está mal*
DEHS-deh mee POON-toh deh VEES-tah loh keh ehs-TAHS dee-see-EHN-doh ehs-TAH mahl

## I don't share your ideas
*No comparto tus ideas*
Noh kohm-PAHR-toh toos ee-DEH-ahs

## Can I say what I think about this?
*¿Puedo decir lo que pienso sobre esto?*
PWEH-doh deh-SEER loh keh pee-EHN-soh SOH-breh EHS-toh

## Yes, of course. Everyone can give their opinion
*Sí, por supuesto. Todo el mundo puede dar su opinión*
See, pohr soo-poo-EHS-toh TOH-doh ehl MOON-doh PWEH-deh dahr soo oh-pee-nee-OHN

## Your opinion is not allowed in this room
*Tu opinión no es bienvenida en esta sala*
Too oh-pee-nee-OHN noh ehs bee-ehn-veh-NEE-dah ehn EHS-tah SAH-lah

## What are your thoughts about this matter?
*¿Qué piensas sobre este tema?*
Keh pee-EHN-sahs SOH-breh EHS-teh TEH-mah

## He offered a controversial opinion
*Ofreció una opinión polémica*
Oh-freh-see-OH OO-nah oh-pee-nee-OHN poh-LEH-mee-kah

## Was I wrong in my theory?
*¿Estaba equivocada con mi teoría?*
Ehs-TAH-bah eh-kee-voh-KAH-dah kohn mee teh-oh REE-ah

Her thoughts created the argument
*Sus ideales crearon una discusión*
Soos ee-deh-AH-lehs kreh-AH-rohn OO-nah dees-koo-see-OHN

Your speech is bothering me
*Tu discurso me está molestando*
Too dees-KOOR-soh meh ehs-TAH moh-lehs-TAHN-doh

Tell me the truth
*Dime la verdad*
DEE-meh lah vehr-DAHD

What makes you think that?
*¿Qué te hace pensar así?*
Keh teh AH-seh pehn-SAHR ah-SEE

You need to open your eyes and see the reality
*Necesitas abrir los ojos y ver la realidad*
Neh-seh-SEE-tahs ah-BREER lohs OH-hohs ee vehr lah reh-ah-lee-DAHD

There is no reason
*No hay ninguna razón*
Noh AH-ee neen-GOO-nah rah-SOHN

He interrupted me when I was talking
*Me interrumpió cuando yo estaba hablando*
Meh een-teh-rroom-pee-OH koo-AHN-doh yoh ehs-TAH-bah ah-BLAHN-doh

# Hotel and Travel

I would like to book a room
*Me gustaría reservar una habitación*
Meh goos-tah-REE-ah rreh-sehr-VAHR OO-nah ah-bee-tah-see-OHN

How much is the room per night?
*¿Cuánto cuesta la habitación por noche?*
KWAHN-toh KWEHS-tah lah ah-bee-tah-see-OHN pohr NOH-cheh

What is the code for the safe of the room?
*¿Cuál es la contraseña de la caja fuerte de la habitación?*
KWAHL ehs lah kohn-trah-SHE-nyah deh lah KAH-hah foo-HER-teh deh lah ah-bee-tah-see-OHN

Can I have a wake-up call?
*¿Pueden llamarme para despertarme?*
PWEH-dehn yah-MAHR-meh PAH-rah dehs-pehr-TAHR-meh

**What time does the breakfast close at?**
*¿A qué hora cierran el desayuno?*
Ah keh OH-rah see-EH-rrahn ehl deh-sah-YOO-noh

**Do you take credit cards?**
*¿Aceptas tarjetas de crédito?*
Ah-SEHP-tahs tahr-HEH-tahs deh KREH-dee-toh

**Can you take a photo of me, please?**
*¿Puedes tomarme una foto, por favor?*
PWEH-dehs toh-MAHR-meh oo-nah foh-toh pohr fa-VOHR

**What sights should I visit?**
*¿Qué lugares debo visitar?*
KEH loo-GAH-rehs DEH-boh vee-see-TAHR

**Where can I get the best local food?**
*¿Dónde puedo conseguir la mejor comida local?*
DOHN-deh PWEH-doh kohn-seh-GEER lah meh-HOR koh-MEE-dah loh-KAHL

**What can I do for fun here?**
*¿Qué puedo hacer para divertirme aquí?*
Keh PWEH-doh ah-SEHR PAH-rah dee-vehr-TEER-meh ah-KEE

**Do we need to get cash?**
*¿Necesitamos dinero en efectivo?*
Neh-seh-see-TAH-mohs dee-NEH-roh ehn eh-fehk-TEE-voh

**It is legal in this country**
*Es legal en este país*
Ehs leh-GAHL ehn EHS-teh pah-EES

**Could you let me know when we arrive...?**
*¿Me puedes avisar cuando lleguemos …?*
Meh ah-VEE-sahs KWAHN-doh yeh-GEH-mohs...

**I would like to hire a bicycle**
*Me gustaría alquilar una bicicleta*
Meh goos-tah-REE-ah ahl-kee-LAHR oo-nah bee-cee-CLEH-tah

**I want to practice my Spanish**
*Quiero practicar mi español*
Kee-EH-roh prahk-tee-KAHR mee ehs-pah-NYOHL

**I would like to change my room**
*Me gustaría cambiar de habitación*
Meh goos-tah-REE-ah kahm-bee-AHR deh ah-bee-tah-see-OHN

**I would like a room with a view**
*Me gustaría una habitación con vista*
Meh goos-tah-REE-ah oo-nah ah-bee-tah-see-OHN kohn VEES-tah

**I would like a cheaper room**
*Me gustaría una habitación más barata*
Meh goos-tah-REE-ah oo-nah ah-bee-tah-see-OHN mahs bah-RAH-tah

**Do you have any double rooms?**
*¿Tienes habitaciones dobles?*
Tee-EH-nehs ah-bee-tah-see-OH-nehs DOH-blehs

**And the front desk?**
*¿Y a recepción?*
ee ah reh-sehp-see-OHN

**Do you have the key to the room?**
*¿Tienes la llave de la habitación?*
Tee-EH-nehs lah YAH-veh deh lah ah-bee-tah-see-OHN

**Do you have any suites?**
*¿Tienes alguna suite?*
Tee-EH-nehs ahl-GOO-nah soo-EET

**How do I call the room service?**
*¿Cómo llamo al servicio de habitaciones?*
KOH-moh YAH-moh ahl sehr-VEE-see-oh deh ah-bee-tah-see-OH-nehs

**Where is the closest coffee shop?**
*¿Dónde está la cafetería más cercana?*
DOHN-deh ehs-TAH lah ka-feh-teh-REE-ah mahs sehr-KAH-nah

**Where can I exchange currency?**
*¿Dónde puedo cambiar dinero?*
DOHN-deh PWEH-doh kahm-bee-AHR dee-neh-roh

**Is that illegal here?**
*¿Esto es ilegal aquí?*
EHS-toh ehs ee-leh-GAHL ah-KEEH

**Can I have an extra pillow please?**
*¿Puede darme una almohada más por favor?*
PWEH-deh DAHR-meh oo-nah ahl-moh-AH-dah mahs pohr fah-VOHR

**Were you born here?**
*¿Has nacido aquí?*
Ahs nah-SEE-doh ah-KEE

**My hotel address is…**
*La dirección de mi hotel es…*
Lah dee-rehk-see-OHN deh mee hoh-TE-HL ehs

**I'm located at…**
*Estoy ubicado en…*
Ehs-TOH-ee oo-bee-KAH-doh ehn

**What is your address?**
*¿Cuál es tu dirección?*
KWAHL ehs too dee-rehk-see-OHN

**When does your flight leave?**
*¿Cuándo sale tu vuelo?*
KWAHN-doh SAH-leh too voo-EH-loh

**I want to cancel my booking**
*Quiero cancelar mi reserva*
Kee-EH-roh kahn-seh-LAHR mee reh-SEHR-vah

**Do you need help?**
*¿Necesitas ayuda?*
Neh-seh-SEE-tahs ah-YOO-dah

# Responses

**We are tourists on vacation**
*Somos turistas de vacaciones*
SOH-mohs too-REES-tahs deh vah-kah-see-OH-nehs

**I am from...**
*Soy de...*
SOH-ee deh

**I am travelling for work**
*Estoy viajando por trabajo*
Ehs-TOH-ee vee-ah-HAHN-doh pohr trah-BAH-hoh

**I am travelling for leisure**
*Estoy viajando por placer*
Ehs-TOH-ee vee-ah-HAHN-doh pohr plah-SEHR

**Hurry up or we will miss the flight**
*Date prisa o perderemos el vuelo*
DAH-teh PREE-sah oh pehr-deh-REH-mohs ehl voo-EH-loh

**I have lost my luggage**
*He perdido mi equipaje*
Eh- pehr-DEE-doh mee eh-kee-PAH-heh

**Sorry, I don't live here**
*Lo siento, no vivo aquí*
Loh see-EHN-toh noh VEE-voh ah-KEE

**I don't have cash**
*No tengo efectivo*
Noh TEHN-goh eh-fehk-TEE-voh

**Your country is beautiful**
*Tu país es hermoso*
Too pah-EES ehs ehr-MOH-soh

**It was a pleasant flight**
*Fue un vuelo agradable*
Foo-EH oon voo-EH-loh ah-grah-DAH-bleh

**I am here for a short stay**
*Estoy aquí por un período corto*
Ehs-TOH-ee ah-KEE pohr oon peh-REEH-oh-doh COHR-toh

**I need to take cash out**
*Tengo que sacar dinero*
TEHN-goh keh sah-KAHR dee-NEH-roh

**I am traveling around the country**
*Estoy viajando por el país*
Ehs-TOH-ee vee-ah-HAHN-doh pohr ehl pah-EES

**I'm lost**
*Estoy perdido*
Ehs-TOH-ee pehr-DEE-doh

**Yes I was born here**
*Si, nací aquí*
see nah-SEEH ah-KEE

**No, I was not born here**
*No, no nací aquí*
Noh noh nah-SEEH ah-KEE

**We are travelling around the world**
*Estamos viajando por el mundo*
Ehs-TAH-mohs vee-ah-HAHN-doh pohr ehl MOON-doh

**Can I have your passport please?**
*¿Me das tu pasaporte por favor?*
Meh dahs too pah-seh-POHR-teh pohr fah-VOHR

**My flight leaves tomorrow evening**
*Mi vuelo sale mañana por la noche*
Mee voo-EH-loh SAH-leh ma-NYAH-nah pohr lah NOH-cheh

**Excuse me, where can I do the check-in here?**
*Perdona, ¿dónde puedo facturar aquí?*
Pehr-DOH-nah DOHN-deh poo-EH-doh fahk-too-RAHR ah-KEE

**Where can I get a taxi?**
*¿Dónde puedo tomar un taxi?*
DOHN-deh PWEH-doh toh-MAHR oon TAHK-see

**Does Uber work here?**
*¿Uber funciona aquí?*
OO-behr foon-see-OH-nah ah-KEE

**I want to write a complaint**
*Quiero escribir una queja*
KEE-eh-roh ehs-kree-BEER oo-nah KEH-hah

**Where can I find this street?**
*¿Dónde puedo encontrar esta calle?*
DOHN-deh PWEH-doh ehn-KOHN-trahr ehs-tah KAH-yeh

**Where can I buy a map?**
*¿Dónde puedo comprar un mapa?*
DOHN-deh PWEH-doh cohm-PRAHR oon MAH-pah

**I come from…**
*Vengo de…*
VEHN-goh deh

**Can you give me a bus schedule?**
*¿Puede darme un horario de bus?*
PWEH-deh DAHR-meh oon oh-RAH-ree-oh deh boos

**I need...**
*Necesito…*
Neh-SEH-see-toh

# Directions

**Where is…?**
*¿Dónde está…?*
DOHN-deh ehs-TAH

**Do you have a map of the city?**
*¿Tienes un mapa de la ciudad?*
Tee-EH-nehs oon MAH-pah deh lah see-oo-DAHD

**Where is the bank?**
*¿Dónde está el banco?*
DOHN-deh ehs-TAH ehl BAHN-koh

**Where's the nearest railway station?**
*¿Dónde está la estación de tren más cercana?*
DOHN-deh ehs-TAH lah ehs-tah-see-OHN deh trehn mahs sehr-KAH-nah

### Where's the nearest bus stop?
*¿Dónde está la parada de autobús más cercana?*
DOHN-deh ehs-TAH lah pah-RAH-dah deh ah-ooh-toh-BOOS mahs sehr-KAH-nah

### A ticket to … please.
*Un ticket para … por favor*
Oon TEE-keht PAH-rah … pohr fah-VOHR

### How much does a ticket to … cost?
*¿Cuánto cuesta un ticket para…?*
KWAHN-toh KWEHS-tah ooh TEE-keht pah-rah

### You can drop me off anywhere here
*Puedes dejarme en cualquier lugar aquí*
PWEH-dehs deh-HAHR-meh ehn koo-ahl-kee-EHR loo-GAHR ah-KEE

### Do you know where … is?
*¿Sabes dónde está…?*
SAH-behs DOHN-deh ehs-TAH

### Is this the right way to…?
*¿Es este el camino correcto hacia…?*
Ehs EHS-teh ehl kah-MEE-noh koh-RREHK-toh hah-SEE-ah

### Where can we find parking around here?
*¿Dónde podemos encontrar aparcamiento por aquí?*
DOHN-deh poh-DEH-mohs ehn-kohn-TRAHR ah-pahr-kah-mee-EHN-toh pohr ah-KEE

### What can we see near our hotel?
*¿Qué podemos ver cerca de nuestro hotel?*
Keh poh-DEH-mohs vehr SEHR-kah deh noo-EHS-troh oh-TEHL

## Responses

### Keep the change
*Quédate con el cambio*
KEH-dah-teh kohn ehl KAHM-bee-oh

### Over there
*Por ahí*
Pohr ah-EE

### Head east
*Ve hacia el este*
Veh AH-see-ah ehl EHS-teh

### Go to the southeast of the city
*Ve hacia el sureste de la ciudad*
Veh AH-see-ah ehl soor-EHS-teh deh lah see-oo-DAHD

### In what direction is south?
*¿En qué dirección está el sur?*
Ehn keh dee-rehk-see-OHN ehs-TAH ehl soor

### The compass always marks the north
*La brújula siempre marca el norte*
Lah BROO-hoo-lah see-EHM-preh MAHR-kah ehl NOHR-teh

**We have visited the west of the country**
*Hemos visitado el oeste del país*
EH-mohs vee-see-TAH-doh ehl oh-EHS-teh dehl pah-EES

**These birds migrate to the northeast**
*Esos pájaros emigran hacia el noreste*
EHS- sohs PAH-hah-rohs eh-MEE-grahn AH-see-ah ehl noh-REHS-teh

**Following the map, we have to go northwest**
*De acuerdo al mapa, tenemos que ir al noroeste*
De a coo er-doh  ahl MAH-pah teh-NEH-mohs keh eer ahl noh-roh-EHS-teh

**Shall we go to the southwest?**
*¿Deberíamos ir al suroeste?*
Deh-beh-REE-ah-mohs eer ahl soo-roh-EHST-teh

**Turn right**
*Gira a la derecha*
HEE-rah ah lah deh-REH-chah

**Turn left**
*Gira a la izquierda*
HEE-rah ah lah ees-kee-EHR-dah

**Go straight**
*Ve recto*
Veh REHK-toh

**It's right here**
*Está justo aquí*
Ehs-TAH HOOS-toh ah-KEE

**I need to go to that place**
*Necesito ir a ese lugar*
Neh-seh-SEE-toh eer ah EH-seh loo-GAHR

**I can't find you**
*No te encuentro*
Noh teh ehn-koo-EHN-troh

**It's behind this building**
*Está detrás de este edificio*
Ehs-TAH deh-TRAHS deh EHS-teh eh-dee-FEE-see-oh

**It's on the other side of the road**
*Está en el otro lado de la  calle*
Ehs-TAH ehn ehl OH-troh LAH-doh deh lah kah- ye

**It is around the corner**
*Está a la vuelta de la esquina*
Ehs-TAH ah lah voo-EHL-tah deh lah ehs-KEE-nah

**I'm on my way**
*Voy de camino*
VOH-ee deh kah-MEE-noh

**You are going the wrong way**
*Vas por el camino equivocado*
Vahs pohr ehl kah-MEE-noh eh-kee-voh-KAH-doh

**We have to cross the road**
*Tenemos que cruzar la  calle*
Teh-NEH-mohs keh kroo-SAHR lah kah- ye

**The museum is in front of that square**
*El museo está en frente de esa plaza*
Ehl moo-SEH-oh ehs-TAH ehn FREHN-teh deh EH-sah PLAH-sah

# Ordering Food and Drinks

**I recommend this restaurant**
*Recomiendo este restaurante*
Reh-koh-mee-EHN-doh EHS-teh rehs-tah-oo-RAHN-teh

**I don't recommend this pub**
*No recomiendo este pub*
Noh reh-koh-mee-EHN-doh EHS-teh poob

**Let's leave a review**
*Vamos a dejar un comentario*
VAH-mohs ah deh-HAHR- oon koh-mehn-TAH-ree-oh

**Can I see the menu?**
*¿Puedo ver el menú?*
PWEH-doh vehr ehl meh-NOO

**Can I get a coaster?**
*¿Puedes darme un posavasos?*
PWEH-dehs DAHR-meh oon poh-sah-VAH-sohs

**Do you want to share a dish?**
*¿Quieres compartir un plato?*
Kee-EH-rehs kohm-pahr-TEER oon PLAH-toh

**Can we see the drinks menu?**
*¿Podemos ver el menú de bebidas?*
Poh-DEH-mohs vehr ehl meh-NOO deh beh-BEE-dahs

**Do you serve alcohol?**
*¿ Sirves alcohol?*
SEER - vehs ahl-koh-OHL

**What is the most popular dish here?**
*¿Cuál es el plato más popular aquí?*
Kwahl ehs ehl PLAH-toh mahs poh-poo-LAHR  ah-KEE

**What are the specials today?**
*¿Cuáles son los especiales del día?*
KWAH-lehs sohn lohs ehs-peh-see-AH-lehs dehl DEE-ah

**What are you going to order?**
*¿Qué vas a pedir?*
Keh   vahs ah peh-DEER

**Where is your bathroom?**
*¿Dónde está el baño?*
DOHN-deh ehs-TAH ehl BAH-nyoh

**We are ready to order**
*Estamos listos para pedir*
Ehs-TAH-mohs LEES-tohs pah-rah peh-DEER

**I would like a coffee please**
*Querría un café por favor*
Keh-RRE-ah oon ka-FEH pohr fah-VOHR

**I would like a decaffeinated coffee please**
*Querría un descafeinado por favor*
Keh-RRE-ah oon dehs-ka-feh-ee-NAH-doh pohr fah-VOHR

Can you please get me some sugar
*¿Puedes traerme un poco de azúcar?*
PWEH-dehs trah-EHR-meh oon POH-koh deh a-SOO-kahr

Extra sugar please
*Más azúcar por favor*
MAHS Ah-SOO-kahr pohr fah-VOHR

No sugar, thanks
*Sin azúcar, gracias*
Seen ah-SOO-kahr GRAH-see-ahs

Can you please get me the salt?
*¿Puedes traerme sal?*
PWEH-dehs trah-EHR-meh sahl

Can you please get me the pepper?
*¿Puedes traerme pimienta?*
PWEH-dehs trah-EHR-meh pee-mee-EHN-tah

Do you eat cereal in the mornings?
*¿Comes cereales por la mañana?*
KOH-mehs seh-reh-AH-lehs pohr lah mah-NYAH-nah

I would like milk in my coffee
*Quisiera leche en mi café*
Kee-see-EH-rah LEH-cheh ehn mee kah-FEH

Do you serve any milk alternatives?
*¿Sirven alternativas a la leche?*
SEER-vehn ahl-tehr-nah-TEE-vahs ah lah LEH-cheh

Do you serve almond milk?
*¿Sirves leche de almendras?*
SEER-vehs LEH-cheh deh ahl-MEHN-drahs

Do you serve soy milk?
*¿Sirves leche de soja?*
SEER-vehs LEH-cheh deh SOH-hah

I would like almond milk in my coffee
*Quisiera leche de almendras en mi café*
Kee-see-EH-rah LEH-cheh deh ahl-MEHN-drahs ehn mee kah-FEH

I would like cream in my coffee
*Quisiera crema en mi café*
Kee-see-EH-rah creh-mah ehn mee kah-FEH

Can you make my dish spicy?
*¿Puedes hacer que mi plato sea picante?*
PWEH-dehs ah-SEHR keh mee PLAH-toh SEH-ah pee-KAHN-teh

Please add some chilli to my food
*Por favor, añade un poco de chilli a mi comida*
Pohr fah-VOHR ah-nyah-deh oon POH-koh deh CHEE-lee ah mee coh-MEH-dah

No spicy dishes please
*Nada de platos picantes por favor*
NAH-dah deh PLAH-tohs pee-KAHN-tehs pohr fah-VOHR

I would like my steak medium rare
*Querría mi bistec jugoso*
Keh-RRE-ah mee bees-TEHK joo-GO-soh

I would like my steak medium.
*Querría mi bistec a punto*
Keh-RRE-ah mee bees-TEHK a POON-toh

I would like my steak well done
*Querría mi bistec bien cocido*
Keh-RRE-ah mee bees-TEHK bee-en-co SEE do

Nothing else, thank you
*Nada más, gracias*
NAH-dah mahs GRAH-see-ahs

I'll have red wine please
*Tomaré vino tinto, por favor*
Toh-mah-REH VEE-noh TEEN-toh pohr fah-VOHR

I'll have white wine please
*Tomaré vino blanco, por favor*
Toh-mah-REH VEE-noh BLAHN koh pohr fah-VOHR

Can you re-fill my glass please?
*¿Puedes rellenar mi vaso por favor?*
PWEH-dehs reh-yeh-NAHR-mee VAH-soh pohr fah-VOHR

Do you serve any vegetarian dishes?
*¿Sirves algún plato vegetariano?*
SEER-vehs al-GOON PLAH-toh veh-heh-tah-ree-AH-noh

Do you serve any dishes for vegans?
*¿Sirves algún plato para veganos?*
SEER-vehs al-GOON PLAH-toh PAH-rah veh-GAH-nohs

Is this gluten free?
*¿Esto es sin gluten?*
EHS-toh ehs seen GLOO-tehn

There are no drinks left
*No quedan bebidas*
Noh KEH-dahn beh-BEE-dahs

I don't eat meat
*No como carne*
Noh KOH-moh KAHR-neh

I feel like I want some fruit
*Me apetece algo de fruta*
Meh ah-peh-TEH-seh AHL-goh deh FROO-tah

Do you like apples or bananas?
*¿Te gustan las manzanas o los plátanos?*
Teh GOOS-tahn lahs mahn-SAH-nahs oh lohs PLAH-tah-nohs

I prefer the peach
Prefiero el durazno
Preh-fee-EH-roh ehl doo-RAHS-no

Pears are disgusting
*Las peras son asquerosas*
Lahs PEH-rahs sohn ahs-keh-ROH-sahs

Oranges are my favourites
*Las naranjas son mis favoritas*
Lahs nah-RAHN-hahs sohn mees fah-voh-REE-tahs

## I don't eat pork
No como cerdo

Noh KOH-moh SEHR-doh

## This burger is made with beef
*Esta hamburguesa está hecha de ternera*

Ehs-tah ahm-boor-GEH-sah ehs-TAH EH-chah deh tehr-NEH-rah

## What do you think of lamb's meat?
*¿Qué piensas de la carne de cordero?*

Keh pee-EHN-sahs deh lah KAHR-neh deh kohr-DEH-roh

## Is there meat in this dish?
*¿Hay carne en este plato?*

AH-ee KAHR-neh ehn EHS-teh PLAH-toh

## What have you got for dessert?
*¿Qué  tienes de postre?*

Keh  tee-EH-nehs deh POHS-treh

## I didn't like the food from here
*No me gustó la comida de aquí*

Noh meh goos-TOH lah koh-MEE-dah deh ah-KEE

## I am allergic to seafood
*Soy alérgico  a los mariscos*

SOH-ee ah-LEHR-hee-koh a lohs mah-REES-kohs

## I am allergic to nuts
*Soy alérgico a los frutos secos*

SOH-ee ah-LEHR-hee-koh ah lohs FROO-tohs SEH-kohs

## I am lactose intolerant
*Soy intolerante a la lactosa*

SOH-ee een-toh-leh-RAHN-teh ah lah lahk-TOH-sah

## Please seat us in the non-smoking section
*Por favor siéntenos en la sección de no fumadores*

Pohr-FAH-vohr see-EHN-teh-nohs ehn lah sehk-see-OHN deh noh foo-mah-DOH-rehs

## Please seat us in the smoking section
*Por favor, siéntenos en la sección de fumadores*

Pohr-FAH-vohr see-EHN-teh-nohs ehn lah sehk-see-OHN deh foo-mah-DOH-rehs

## Can we be seated inside?
*¿Podemos sentarnos dentro?*

Poh-DEH-mohs sehn-TAHR-nohs DEHN-troh

## Can we be seated outside?
*¿Podemos sentarnos fuera?*

Poh-DEH-mohs sehn-TAHR-nohs FWEH-rah

## I need one more sit
*Necesito un asiento más*

Neh-seh-SEE-toh oon ah-see-EHN-toh mahs

## Is this dish spicy?
*¿Este plato es picante?*

EHS-teh PLAH-toh ehs pee-KAHN-teh

This is an Italian restaurant
*Esto es un restaurante italiano*
EHS-toh ehs oon rehs-tah-oo-RAHN-teh
ee-tah-lee-AH-noh

I thought you served Spanish food
*Pensé que servían comida española*
Pehn- SEH keh sehr-VEE-ahn koh-MEE-dah ehs-pah-NYOH-lah

They love chinese food
*Les encanta la comida china*
Lehs ehn-KAHN-tah lah koh-MEE-dah CHEE-nah

I prefer Indian food
*Yo prefiero la comida Hindú*
Yoh preh-dee-EH-roh lah koh-MEE-dah een- DOOH

Fast food is not healthy
*La comida rápida no es saludable*
Lah koh-MEE-dah RAH-pee-dah noh ehs sah-looh-DAH-bleh

Mediterranean diet is a blessing
*La dieta mediterránea es una bendición*
Lah dee-EH-tah meh-dee-teh-RRAH-neh-ah ehs OO-nah behn-dee-see-OHN

It was delicious
*Estaba delicioso*
Ehs-TAH-bah dch lee-see-OH-soh

Can I get this to go, please?
*¿Puedes ponerlo para llevar, por favor?*
PWEH-dehs poh-NEHR-loh PAH-rah yeh-VAHR pohr fah-VOHR

What time do you close?
*¿A qué hora cierras?*
Ah keh OH-rah seeh-eRRAH-s

What time does the kitchen close?
*¿A qué hora cierra la cocina?*
Ah keh OH-rah see-EH-rrah lah koh-SEE-nah

What time does the bar close?
*¿A qué hora cierra el bar?*
Ah keh OH-rah see-EH-rrah eehl bahr

Please clear the table
*Por favor, limpia la mesa*
Pohr fah-VOHR LEEM-pee-ah lah MEH-sah

May we have the bill, please?
*¿Puede traernos la cuenta por favor?*
PWEH-deh trah-EHR-nohs lah KWEHN-tah pohr fah-VOHR

I want a complaint form
*Quiero la hoja de reclamaciones*
Kee-EH-roh lah OH-hah deh reh-klah-mah-see-OH-nehs

Are the toilets clean?
*¿Están limpios los baños?*
Ehs-TAHN LEEM-pee-ohs lohs BAH - nee - ohs

# Jobs

**What do you do for a living?**
*¿En qué trabajas?*
Ehn keh trah-BAH-hahs

**Where do you work?**
*¿Dónde trabajas?*
DOHN-deh trah-BAH-hahs

**Where is your office?**
*¿Dónde está tu oficina?*
DOHN-deh ehs-TAH too oh-fee-SEE-nah

**What industry are you in?**
*¿En qué industria estás?*
Ehn keh een-DOOS-tree-ah ehs-TAHS

**What is the name of your company?**
*¿Cuál es el nombre de tu empresa?*
KWAHL ehs ehl NOHM-breh deh too ehm-PREH-sah

**What company do you work for?**
*¿Para qué compañía trabajas?*
PAH-rah keh kohm-pah-NEE-ah trah-BAH-hahs

**How long have you been working at your company for?**
*¿Cuánto tiempo llevas trabajando en tu empresa?*
KUAHN-toh tee-EHM-poh YEH-vahs ehn too ehm-PREH-sah

**Do you have a business card?**
*¿Tienes una tarjeta de visitas?*
Tee-EH-nehs OO-nah tahr-HEH-tah deh vee-SEE-thas

**Are you hiring?**
*¿Estás contratando?*
Ehs-TAHS kohn-trah-TAHN-doh

**I would like to talk to the boss**
*Me gustaría hablar con el jefe*
Meh goos-tah-REE-ah ah-BLAHR kohn ehl HEH-feh

**Are you looking for a job?**
*¿Estás buscando trabajo?*
Ehs-TAHS boos-KAHN-doh trah-BAH-hoh

**Can I leave my CV?**
*¿Puedo dejar mi curriculum?*
PWEH-doh deh-HAHR mee coo-RREE-coo-loom

**What are your hobbies?**
*¿Cuáles son tus aficiones?*
KWAH-lehs sohn toos ah-fee-see-OH-nehs

**Can we set up a meeting?**
*¿Podemos organizar una reunión?*
Poh-DEH-mohs ohr-gah-nee-SAHR OO-nah reh-oo-nee-OHN

34

How many days do you work during the week?
*¿Cuántos días trabajas durante la semana?*
KWAHN-tohs DEE-ahs trah-BAH-hahs doo-RAHN-the lah she-MAH-nah

Do you work in the weekends?
*¿Trabajas los fines de semana?*
Trah-BAH-hahs lohs FEE-nehs deh she-MAH-nah

What is your availability?
*¿Cuál es tu disponibilidad?*
KWAHL ehs too dees-poh-nee-bee-lee-DAHD

Do you have the night shift?
*¿Tienes el turno nocturno?*
Tee-EH-nehs ehl TOOR-noh noc-TOOR-noh

Do you have the day shift?
*¿Tienes el turno diurno?*
Tee-EH-nehs ehl TOOR-noh dee-OOR-noh

When do you have your break?
*¿Cuándo tienes el descanso?*
KWAHN-doh tee-EH-nehs ehl dehs-KAHN-soh

Are you working remotely?
*¿Estás trabajando desde casa?*
Ehs-TAHS trah-bah-HAHN-doh DE-HS-deh KAH-sah

We have the interview tomorrow
*Tenemos la entrevista mañana*
Teh-NEH-mohs lah ehn-treh-VEES-tah ma-NYAH-nah

I'll be working late tonight
*Trabajaré hasta tarde esta noche*
trah-bah-hah-REH AHS-tah TAHR-deh EHS-tah NOH-cheh

I'll be leaving early today
*Me iré temprano hoy*
Meh ee-REH tehm-PRAH-noh OH-ee

I want to leave my job and travel the world
*Quiero dejar mi trabajo y viajar por el mundo*
Kee-eh-roh deh-HAHR mee trah-BAH-hoh ee - veea – HAR – por – el –MOON - doh

I got a temporary contract
*Tengo un contrato temporal*
TEHN-goh oon trah-BAH-hoh tehm-poh-RAHL

I have signed a permanent contract
*He firmado un contrato permanente*
Eh feer-MAH-doh oon kohn-TRAH-toh pehr-mah-NEHN-teh

It is a part-time job
*Es un trabajo a media jornada*
Ehs oon trah-BAH-hoh ah MEH-dee-ah hohr-NAH-dah

It is a full-time job
*Es un trabajo a jornada completa*
Ehs oon trah-BAH-hoh ah hohr-NAH-dah kohm-PLEH-tah

I quit my job
*Dejo mi trabajo*
DEH-hoh mee trah-BAH-hoh

35

### Book days off work
*Toma días de descanso*
TOH-mah- DEE-az-deh-des CAN soh

### This is my dream job
*Este es mi trabajo soñado*
EHS-teh ehs mee trah-BAH-hoh soh-NYAH-doh

### I received a call this morning about my business
*He recibido una llamada esta mañana sobre mi negocio*
Eh reh-see-BEE-doh OO-nah yah-MAH-dah EHS-tah mah-NYAH-nah SOH-breh mee neh-GOH-see-oh

### I will ask for help to one of my colleagues
*Pediré ayuda a alguno de mis compañeros*
Peh-dee-REH ah-YOO-dah ah ahl-GOO-nah deh mees kohm-pah-NYEH-rohs

### I get on well with my colleagues
*Me llevo bien con mis compañeros*
Meh YEH-voh bee-EHN kohn mees kohm-pah-NYEH-rohs

# Professions

### I am a teacher
*Soy maestro*
SOH-ee mah-EHS-troh

### I am a gardener
*Soy jardinero*
SOH-ee hahr-dee-NEH-roh

### I am a musician
*Soy músico*
SOH-ee MOO-seh-koh

### I am a doctor
*Soy doctor*
SOH-ee dohk-TOHR

### I am an artist
*Soy artista*
SOH-ee ahr-TEES-tah

### I work for the critical care in the hospital
*Trabajo para cuidados intensivos del hospital*
Trah-BAH-hoh PAH-rah koo-ee-DAH-dohs een-tehn-SEE-vohs dehl ohs-pee-TAHL

### I am a nurse in the hospital
*Soy enfermero en el hospital*
SOH-ee ehn-fehr-MEH-roh ehn ehl ohs-pee-TAHL

### We should call the firefighters
*Deberíamos llamar a los bomberos*
Deh-beh-REE-ah-mohs yah-MAHR ah lohs bohm-BEH-rohs

**I work for the police**
*Trabajo para la policía*
Trah-BAH-hoh PAH-rah lah poh-lee-SEE-ah

**I am an employee from the Government**
*Soy empleado del Gobierno*
SOH-ee ehm-pleh-AH-doh dehl goh-bee-EHR-noh

**He works as a security guard in a parking**
*Trabaja como guardia de seguridad en un aparcamiento*
Trah-BAH-hah KOH-moh goo-AHR-dee-ah deh seh-goo-ree-DAHD ehn oon ah-pahr-kah-mee-EHN-toh

**I work in construction**
*Trabajo en la construcción*
Trah-BAH-hoh ehn lah kohns-trook-see-OHN

**She is a dressmaker**
*Ella es una modista*
EH-yah ehs OO-nah moh-DEES-tah

**I am a businesswoman**
*Soy una mujer de negocios*
SOH-ee OO-nah moo-HEHR deh neh-GOH-see ohs

**We collaborate with a marketing company**
*Colaboramos con una compañía de marketing*
Koh-lah-boh-RAH-mohs kohn OO-nah Kohm-pah-NYAH deh MAHR-keh-teen

**I work in the sales section**
*Trabajo en la sección ventas*
Trah-BAH-hoh ehn lah sehk-see-OHN VEHN-tahs

**My company recruits cleaners**
*Mi compañía contrata limpiadores*
Mee kohm-pah-NYAH kohn-TRAH-tah leem-pee-sh-DOH-rehs

**I wish I were an astronaut**
*Ojalá fuese un astronauta*
oh-hah-LAH foo-EH-seh oon ahs-troh-NAHW-tah

**I have to go to the butcher**
*Tengo que ir al carnicero*
TEHN-goh keh eer ahl kahr-nee-SEH-roh

**I work in a laboratory**
*Trabajo en un laboratorio*
Trah-BAH-hoh eh noon lah-boh-rah-TOH-ree-oh

**I am a journalist**
*Soy periodista*
SOH-ee peh-ree-oh-DEES-tah

**She works as a personal trainer**
*Ella trabaja como entrenadora personal*
EH-yah trah-BAH-hah KOH-moh ehn-treh-nah-DOH-rah pehr-soh-NAHL

**A photographer would have a better camera**
*Un fotógrafo tendría una cámara mejor*
Oon foh-TOH-grah-foh then-DREE-ah OO-nah KAH-mah-rah meh-HOHR

**The receptionist at this hotel is nice**
*La recepcionista de este hotel es simpática*
Lah reh-sehp-see-oh-NEES-tah deh EHS-the oh-TEHL ehs seem-PAH-tee-kah

## I am an electrician
*Soy electricista*
SOH-ee eh-lehk-tree-SEES-tah

## This bread is from the baker next door
*Este pan es del panadero de aquí al lado*
EHS-teh pahn ehs dehl pah-nah-DEH-roh deh a KEE ahl LAH-doh

## I am a pilot
*Soy piloto*
SOH-ee pee-LOH-toh

## He is the new politician
*Él es el nuevo político*
El ehs ehl noo-EH-voh poh-LEE-tee-koh

## We should call a travel guide
*Deberíamos llamar a una guía turística (female)*
Deh-beh-REE-ah-mohs yah-MAHR ah OO-nah GEE-ah too-REES-tee-kah

## We should call a travel guide
*Deberíamos llamar un guía turístico (male)*
Deh-beh-REE-ah-mohs yah-MAHR ah OO-nah GEE-ah too-REES-tee-koh

## I am a plumber
*Soy fontanero*
SOH-ee fohn-tah-NEH-roh

## I am a cashier in this supermarket
*Soy una cajera en este supermercado*
SOH-ee OO-nah kah-HEH-rah ehn EHS-teh soo-pehr-mehr-KAH-doh

## The architect should come now
*El arquitecto debería venir ahora*
Ehl ahr-kee-TEHK-toh deh-beh-REE-ah veh-NEER ah-OH-rah

## They know the cook of this restaurant
*Conocen al cocinero de este restaurante*
Koh-NOH-sehn ahl koh-see-NEH-roh deh EHS-the rehs-tah-oh-RAHN-the

## Do you know the waiter?
*¿Conoces al camarero?*
Koh-NOH-sehs ahl kah-mah-REH-roh

## That company is looking for IT consultants
*Esa empresa está buscando consultores de informática*
EH-sah Kohm-pah-NYAH ehs-TAH boos-KAHN-doh kohn-sool-TOH-rehs deh een-fohr-MAH-tee-kah

## We are a group of writers
*Somos un grupo de escritores*
SOH-mohs oon GROO-poh de ehs-cree-TOH-rehs

## Maybe you need a psychologist
*Quizás necesitas un psicólogo*
Kee-SAHS neh-she-SEE-tahs oon see-KOH-loh-goh

## I am the accountant of this shop
*Soy el contable de esta tienda*
SOH-ee ehl kohn-TAH-bleh deh EHS-tah tee-EHN-dah

**When do you go to the hair-dresser?**
*¿Cuándo vas a la peluquería?*
KWAHN-doh vahs ah lah peh-loo-keh-REE-ah

**I am an engineer**
*Soy ingeniero*
SOH-ee een-heh-nee-EH-roh

**You will need a lawyer**
*Necesitarás un abogado*
Neh-she-see-tah-RAHS oon ah-boh-GAH-doh

**I work for the armed forces**
*Trabajo para las fuerzas armadas*
Trah-BAH-hoh PAH-rah lahs foo-HER-sahs ahr-MAH-dahs

**She is a theater actress**
*Ella es una actriz de teatro*
EH-yah ehs OO-nah ahk-TREES deh the-AH-troh

**The car's problem requires a mechanic to fix it**
*El problema del coche requiere un mecánico para arreglarlo*
Ehl proh-BLEH-mah dehl KOH-cheh reh-kee-EH-reh oon meh-KAH-nee-koh PAH-rah ah-rreh-GLAHR-loh

# Hobbies

**What do you do for fun?**
*¿Qué haces para divertirte?*
Keh AH-sehs PAH-rah dee-vehr-TEER-teh

**What book do you recommend to me?**
*¿Qué libro me recomiendas?*
Keh LEE-broh meh reh-koh-mee-EHN-dahs

**Do you play an instrument?**
*¿Tocas algún instumento?*
TOH-kahs ahl-GOON eens-troo-MEHN-toh

**Did you buy a new yoga mat?**
*¿ Compraste una esterilla de yoga nueva?*
Teh kohm-PRAHS-teh OO-nah ehs-teh-REE-yah deh YOH-gah noo-EH-vah

**My favourite sport is soccer**
*Mi deporte favorito es el fútbol*
Mee deh-POHR-teh fah-voh-REE-to ehs ehl FOOT-bohl

**I love to dance**
*Me encanta bailar*
Meh ehn-KAHN-tah bah-ee-LAHR

**Fishing is my favourite activity**
*Pescar es mi actividad favorita*
Pehs-CAHR ehs mee ahk-tee-vee-DAHD fah-voh-REE-tah

**I play guitar in my spare time**
*Toco la guitarra en mi tiempo libre*
TOH-coh lah gee-TAH-rrah ehn mee tee-EHM-poh LEE-breh

**I am a runner**
*Soy corredor*
SOH-ee koh-rreh-DOHR

**Where is the closest casino?**
*¿Dónde está el casino más cercano?*
DOHN-deh ehs-TAH ehl kah-SEH-noh mahs sehr-KAH-noh

**I like painting in my free time**
*Me gusta pintar en mi tiempo libre*
Meh GOOS-tah peen-TAHR ehn mee tee-EHM-poh LEE-breh

**We watch that tv program every night**
*Vemos ese programa de tele-visión todas las noches*
BEH-mohs EH-seh proh-GRAH-mah deh teh-leh-vee-see-OHN TOH-dahs lahs NOH-chehs

**He plays the piano when he has time**
*El toca el piano cuando tiene tiempo*
EL TOH-kah ehl pee-AH-noh koo-AHN-doh tee-EH-neh tee-EHM-poh

**I enjoyed that book**
*Disfruté ese libro*
Dees-froo-TEH EH-seh LEE-broh

**I play the guitar in a band**
*Toco la guitarra en una banda*
TOH-koh lah gee-TAH-rrah ehn OO-nah BAHN-dah

**We are members of an orchestra**
*Somos miembros de una orquesta*
SOH-mohs mee-EHM-brohs deh OO-nah ohr-KEHS-tah

**I get riding lessons**
*Doy clases de equitación*
DOH-ee KLAH-sehs deh eh-kee-tah-see-OHN

**I like children that and I am a babysitter**
*Me gustan los niños y soy niñera*
Meh GOOS-tahn lohs NEE-nyos ee SOH-ee nee-NYEH-rah

**I do crafts for fun**
*Hago manualidades por di-versión*
AH-goh mah-noo-ah-lee-DAH-dehs pohr dee-vehr-see-OHN

**We practise magic together**
*Practicamos magia juntos*
Prahk-tee-KAH-mohs MAH-hee-ah HOON-tohs

**I do meditation after work**
*Hago meditación después del trabajo*
AH-goh meh-dee-tah-see-OHN dehs-poo-EHS dehl trah-BAH-hoh

**I have a farm to go during the weekends**
*Tengo una granja para ir los fines de semana*
TEHN-OO-nah GRAHN-hah PAH-rah eer lohs FEE-nehs deh seh-MAH-nah

### I walk dogs in the afternoon
*Paseo perros por las tardes*
Pah-SEH-oh PEH-rrohs pohr lahs
TAHR-dehs

### They volunteer in an organization
*Son voluntarios en una organización*
Sohn voh-loon-TAH-ree-ohs ehn OO-nah
ohr-gah-nee-sah-see-OHN

### I think that wine tasting is very interesting
*Creo que catar vinos es muy interesante*
KREH-oh keh kah-TAHR VEE-nohs ehs
MOO-ee een-the-reh-SAHN-teh

### We spend time doing sudokus
*Pasamos el tiempo haciendo sudokus*
Pah-SAH-mohs ehl tee-EHM-poh ah-see-
EHN-doh soo-DOH-koos

### I love cleaning
*Me encanta limpiar*
Meh ehn-KAHN-tah leem-pee-AHR

### Sometimes, I do photo shoots
*A veces hago saco fotos*
Ah VEH-sehs SAH - coh - FOH - tohs

### I do video editing in the evenings
*Hago edición de video por las noches*
AH-goh eh-dee-see-OHN deh VEE-deh-
oh pohr lahs NOH-chehs

### I enjoy so much doing my makeup
*Disfuto mucho maquillándome*
Dees-FROO-toh MOO-choh mah-kee-
YAHN-doh-meh

### I don't enjoy writing poetry
*No disfruto escribiendo poesía*
Noh dees-FROO-toh ehs-kree-bee-EHN-
doh poh-eh-SEE-ah

### But I like reading blogs
*Pero me gusta leer blogs*
PEH-roh meh GOOS-tah leh-HER blohgs

### I am good at giving advice
*Soy bueno dando consejos*
SOH-ee boo-EH-noh DAHN-doh kohn-
SHE-hohs

### We do puzzles every month
*Hacemos puzzles cada mes*
Ah-SEH-mohs POOS-lehs KAH-dah
mehs

### She sings pretty well
Ella canta bastante bien
EH-yah KAHN-tah bahs-TAHN-teh
bee-EHN

### Drawing is my passion
*Dibujar es mi pasión*
Dee-boo-HAHR ehs mee pah-see-OHN

### Gaming is an expensive hobby
*Los videojuegos son un pasatiempo caro*
Lohs vee-deh-oh-hoo-EH-gohs soh noon
pah-sah-tee-EHM-poh CAH-roh

### Last weekend we went rock climbing together
*El fin de semana pasado nos fuimos de escalada juntos*
Ehl feen deh seh-MAH-nah nohs foo-EE
mohs deh ehs-kah-LAH-dah HOON-tohs

### The best hobby is travelling
*El mejor pasatiempo es viajar*
Ehl meh-HOHR pah-sah-tee-EHM-poh
ehs vee-ah-HAHR

### We should go to the cinema
*Deberíamos ir al cine*
Deh-beh-REE-ah-mohs eehr ahl SEE-neh

### I don't enjoy action films
*No disfuto viendo películas de acción*
Noh dees-FROO-toh vee-EHN-doh peh-LEE-koo-lahs deh ak-see-OHN

### I enjoy watching horror films
*Disfruto viendo películas de miedo*
Dees-FROO-toh vee-EHN-doh peh-LEE-koo-lahs deh mee-EH-doh

### What do you think of comedies?
*¿Qué piensas de las comedias?*
Keh pee-EHN-sahs deh lahs koh-MEH-dee-ahs

### I prefer films about adventures
*Prefiero las películas de aventuras*
Preh-fee-EH-roh lahs peh-LEE-koo-lahs deh ah-vehn-TOO-rahs

### I hate romantic films
*Odio las películas romántic.*
OH-dee-oh lahs peh-LEE-koo-lahs r
MAHN-tee-kahs

### What about mystery films?
*¿Y las películas de misterio?*
Ee lahs peh-LEE-koo-lahs deh mees-TEH-ree-oh

### I listen to music
*Escucho música*
Ehs-KOO-choh MOO-see-kah

### Do you mean relaxing music?
*¿Quieres decir música relajante?*
Kee-EH-rehs deh-SEER MOO-see-kah
reh-lah-HAHN-the

### I mean classical music
*Quiero decir música clásica*
Kee-EH-roh deh-SEER MOO-see-kah
KLAH-see-kah

### Once a week, I have a long bath
*Una vez a la semana, me doy un baño largo*
OO-nah vehs ah lah she-MAH-nah meh
DOH-ee oon BAH-nyoh LAHR-goh

## Dating

### Table for two, please
*Mesa para dos por favor*
MEH-sah PAH-rah dohs pohr fah-VOHR

### You look beautiful
*Estás hermosa*
Ehs-TAHS ehr-MOH-sah

### Call me
*Llámame*
YAH-mah-meh

### I like you
*Me gustas*
Meh GOOS-tahs

**I like your smile**
*Me gusta tu sonrisa*
Meh GOOS-tah too sohn-RREE-sah

**I'll pick you up tonight**
*Te recojo esta noche*
Teh reh-KOH-ho EHS-tah NOH-cheh

**Do you want anything to drink?**
*¿Quieres algo de beber?*
Kee-EH-rehs AHL-goh deh beh-BEHR?

**Let me get that for you**
*Déjame ayudarte con eso*
DEH-hah-meh ah-yoo-DAHR-teh kohn EH-soh

**Are you having a good time?**
*¿Lo estás pasando bien?*
Loh ehs-TAHS pah-SAHN-doh bee-EHN

**We can dance all night**
*Podemos bailar toda la noche*
Poh-DEH-mohs bah-ee-LAHR TOH-dah lah NOH-cheh

**Do you want to show me around your city?**
*¿Quieres mostrarme tu ciudad?*
Kee-EH-rehs mohs-TRAHR-meh too see-oo-DAHD

**Would you go on a date with me?**
*¿Tendrías una cita conmigo?*
Tehn-DREE-ahs OO-nah SEE-tah kohn-MEE-goh

**What is your phone number?**
*¿Cuál es tu número de teléfono?*
Koo-AHL ehs too NOO-meh-roh deh teh-LEH-foh-noh

**I'm looking for something with no strings attached**
*Estoy buscando algo sin compromiso*
Ehs-TOH-ee boos-KAHN-doh AHL-goh seen com – pro – MEE - soh

**Our relationship is working**
*Nuestra relación funciona*
Noo-EHS-trah reh-lah-see-OHN foon-see-OH-nah

**Stay here tonight**
*Quédate aquí esta noche*
KEH-dah-teh ah-KEE EHS-tah NOH-cheh

**I'm looking for love**
*Estoy buscando el amor*
Ehs-TOH-ee boos-KAHN-doh ehl ah-MOHR

**Happy Saint Valentine**
*Feliz San Valentín*
Feh-LEES sahn vah-lehn-TEEN

**Of all the gifts, your love is the best one**
*De todos los regalos, tu amor es el mejor*
Deh TOH-dohs lohs reh-GAH-lohs too ah-MOHR ehs ehl meh-HOHR

**Love doubles happiness and cuts anguish in a half**
*El amor multiplica la felicidad y corta la miseria por la mitad*
Ehl ah-MOHR mool-tee-PLEE-kah lah feh-lee-see-DAHD ee KOHR-tah lah mee-SEH-ree-ah pohr lah mee-TAHD

**I miss you**
*Te echo de menos*
Teh EH-choh deh MEH-nohs

## Let's make a wish together
*Vamos a pedir un deseo juntos*
VAH-mohs ah peh-DEER oon deh-SEH-
oh HOON-tohs

## Would you like me to walk you home?
*¿Quieres que te acompañe a casa?*
Kee-EH-rehs keh teh ah-kohm-PAH-nyeh
ah KAH-sah

## Did you enjoy everything?
*¿Te ha gustado todo?*
Teh ah goos-TAH-doh TOH-doh

## When can I see you again?
*¿Cuándo puedo volver a verte?*
KWAHN-doh poo-EH-doh vohl-VEHR
ah VEHR-teh

## We should spend more time together
*Deberíamos pasar más tiempo juntos*
Deh-beh-REE-ah-mohs pah-SAHR mahs
tee-EHM-poh HOON-tohs

## Can I give you a hug?
*¿Puedo darte un abrazo?*
PWEH-doh DAHR-teh oon ah-BRAH-
soh

## What do you look for in a person?
*¿Qué buscas en una persona?*
Keh BOOS-kahs ehn OO-nah pehr-SOH-
nah

# Responses

## I want to take things slow
*Quiero tomarme las cosas con calma*
Kee-EH-roh toh-MAHR-meh lahs KOH-
sahs kohn KAHL-mah

## My phone number is…
*Mi número de teléfono es…*
Mee NOO-meh-roh deh teh-LEH-foh-
noh ehs

## You're funny!
*¡Eres divertido!*
EH-rehs dee-vehr-TEE-doh

## I had an affair during my marriage
*Tuve un romance durante mi matrimonio*
TOO-veh oon roh-MAHN-seh doo-
RAHN-teh mee mah-tree-MOH-nee-oh

## Unfortunately, I must say no
*Desafortunadamente, debo decir no*
Dehs-ah-fohr-too-nah-dah-MEHN-teh
DEH-boh deh-SEER noh

## I am single
*Estoy soltero*
Ehs-TOH-ee sohl-TEH-roh

## I am only looking for sex
*Solo busco sexo*
SOH-loh BOOS-koh SEK-soh

## I need a break
*Necesito un tiempo*
Neh-seh-SEE-toh oon tee-EHM-poh

44

**I don't like you**
*No me gustas*
Noh meh GOOS-tahs

**I like your style**
*Me gusta tu estilo*
Meh GOOS-tah too ehs-TEE-loh

**Let's get a drink and we'll see**
*Vamos a tomar algo y ya veremos*
VAH-mohs ah toh-MAHR AHL-goh ee yah veh-REH-mohs

**I am 30 years old**
*Tengo 30 años*
TEHN-goh 30 AH-n nee ohs

**Yes, I would like to see you again**
*Sí, me gustaría volver a verte*
See meh goos-tah-REE-ah vohl-VEHR ah vehr-teh

**I don't think we should see each other anymore**
*No creo que debamos vernos más*
Noh KREH-oh keh deh-BAH-mohs VEHR-nohs mahs

**I have been thinking about you**
*He estado pensando en ti*
Eh ehs-TAH-doh pehn-SAHN-doh ehn tee

**I have a boyfriend / girlfriend**
*Tengo novio / novia*
TEHN-goh NOH-vee-oh / NOH-vee-ah

**You have cheated on me**
*Me has engañado*
Meh ahs ehn-gah-NYAH-doh

**Do you want to be with me?**
*¿Quieres ser mi pareja?*
Kee-EH-rehs sehr mee pah-REH-hah

**It was my decision to end this**
*Fue mi decisión acabar con esto*
Foo-EH mee deh-see-see-OHN ah-kah-BAHR kohn EHS-toh

**We gave back the presents to each other**
*Nos dimos los regalos de vuelta*
Nohs DEE-mohs lohs reh-GAH-lohs deh voo-EHL-tah

**I miss my ex boyfriend**
*Echo de menos a mi exnovio*
EH-choh deh MEH-nohs ah mee eks-NOH-vee-oh

**I feel the same for you**
*Siento lo mismo por ti*
See-EHN-toh loh MEES-moh pohr tee

**There is a big difference between you and her**
*Hay una gran diferencia entre tú y ella*
AH-ee OO-nah grahn dee-feh-REHN-see-ah EHN-treh too ee EH-yah

**I love every part of you**
*Me encanta cada parte de ti*
Meh ehn-KAHN-tah KAH-dah PAHR-teh deh tee

**It could be better**
*Podría ser mejor*
Poh-DREE-ah sehr meh-HOHR

45

# Dealing with Obnoxious People

Stop bothering me please
*Deja de molestarme por favor*
DEH-hah deh moh-lehs-TAHR-meh POR
fah-VOHR

Please stop following me
*Por favor, deja de seguirme*
Pohr fah-VOHR DEH-hah deh seh-
GEER-meh

Please be quiet, you are talking loudly
*Por favor, cállate, estás hablan-
do muy fuerte*
Pohr fah-VOHR KAH-yah-teh ehs-TAHS
ah-BLAHN-doh  MOO EE – FOOER
- teh

Can you please turn the volume down?
*Por favor, ¿puedes bajar el vol-
umen?*
Pohr fah-VOHR PWEH-dehs bah-HAHR
ehl voh-LOO-mehn

Please switch the music off, it is too loud
*Por favor apaga la música, está
demasiado alta*
Pohr fah-VOHR ah-PAH-gah lah MOO-
see-kah ehs-TAH deh-mah-see-AH-doh
AHL-tah

Don't ask me again, please
Por favor, no me vuelvas a preguntar.
Pohr fah-VOHR, noh meh voo-EHL-vahs
ah preh-goon-TAHR

I'm not paying for that
No voy a pagar por eso.
Noh VOH-ee ah pah-GAHR pohr EH-
soh

Leave me alone or I am calling the police
*Déjame en paz o llamaré a la
policía*
DEH-hah-meh ehn pahs oh yah-mah-
REH ah lah poh-lee-SEE-ah

You are being very rude
*Estás siendo muy grosero*
Ehs-TAHS see-EHN-doh MOO-ee groh-
SEH-roh

Please stop swearing
*Por favor deja de maldecir*
Pohr fah-VOHR DEH-hah deh mahl-deh-
SEER

Please do not curse around my children
*Por favor no maldigas delante
de mis hijos*
Pohr fah-VOHR noh mahl-DEE-gahs
deh-LAHN-teh deh mees EE-hohs

**Stay away from me!**
*¡Aléjate de mí!*
Ah-LEH-hah-teh deh meeh

**You have tried to rob me!**
*¡Has tratado de robarme!*
Ahs trah-TAH-doh deh roh-BAHR-meh

**Please stop interrupting me**
*Por favor, deja de interrum-*
*pirme*
Pohr fah-VOHR DEH-hah deh een-teh-
rroom-PEHR-meh

**Please do not take pictures of**
**me**
*Por favor, no me hagas fotos*
Pohr fah-VOHR noh meh AH-gahs FOH-
tohs

**Let go of me!**
*¡Suéltame!*
Soo-EHL-tah-meh

**No way! Stop!**
*¡De ninguna manera! ¡Para!*
Deh neen-GOO-nah mah-NEH-rah PAH-
rah

**Please lower your voice**
*Por favor baja la voz*
Pohr fah-VOHR BAH-hah lah vohs

**I am very disappointed in the**
**way you are behaving**
*Estoy muy decepcionado con*
*tu comportamiento*

Ehs-TOH-ee MOO-ee deh-sehp-see-
oh-NAH-doh HOHN- TOO - kohm
pohrtah-mee-EHN-toh

*Ahora no, gracias*
Ah-OH-rah noh GRAH-see-ahs

**What is that horrible noise?**
*¿Qué es ese ruido tan horrible?*
Keh ehs EH-seh roo-EE-doh tahn oh-
RREE-bleh

**Sorry Sir, that is forbidden here**
*Lo siento Señor, eso está prohi-*
*bido aquí*
Loh see-EHN-toh seh-NYOHR EH-soh
ehs-TAH proh-ee-BEE-doh ah-KEE

**I will sue you**
*Te denunciaré*
Teh deh-noon-see-ah-REH

**What you are doing is against**
**the law**
*Lo que estás haciendo va en*
*contra de la ley*
Loh keh ehs-TAHS ah-see-EHN-doh vah
ehn KOHN-trah deh lah LEH-ee

**Don't you dare touch her again!**
*¡No te atrevas a tocarla otra*
*vez!*
Noh teh ah-TREH-vahs ah toh-KAHR-lah
OH-trah vehs

**You are an abuser**
*Eres un maltratador*
EH-rehs oon mahl-trah-tah-DOHR

47

# Shopping and Money

**How much does this cost?**
*¿Cuánto cuesta esto?*
KWAHN-toh KWEHS-tah EHS-toh

**Is that your final price?**
*¿Ese es tu precio final?*
EH-seh ehs too preh-SEE-oh fee-NAHL

**What's your best price?**
*¿Cuál es tu mejor precio?*
KWAL ehs too meh-HOHR PREH-see-oh

**That's too expensive!**
*¡Eso es demasiado caro!*
EH-soh ehs deh-mah-see-AH-doh KAH-roh

**That's very cheap!**
*¡Eso es muy barato!*
EH-soh ehs MOO-ee bah-RAH-toh

**Do you offer a 10% cash discount?**
*¿Ofreces un 10% de descuento en efectivo?*
Oh-FREH-sehs oon 10% deh dehs-koo-EHN-toh ehn eh-fehk-TEE-voh

**Can I get a 10% discount please?**
*¿Puedo obtener un 10% de descuento, por favor?*
PWEH-doh ohb-teh-NEHR oon 10% deh dehs-koo-EHN-toh pohr fah-VOHR

**Is your price negotiable?**
*¿Su precio es negociable?*
Soo PREH-see-oh ehs neh-goh-see-AH-bleh

**Can you deliver this to my hotel?**
*¿Puedes llevar esto a mi hotel?*
PWEH-dehs yeh-VAHR EHS-toh ehn mee oh-TEHL

**Can you gift wrap that please?**
*¿Puedes envolverlo para regalo, por favor?*
PWEH-dehs ehn-vohl-VEHRloh PAH-rah reh-GAH-lo pohr fah-VOHR

**I'm looking for a fully furnished apartment**
*Estoy buscando un apartamento completamente amueblado*
Ehs-TOH-ee boos-KAHN-doh oon ah-pahr-tah-MEHN-toh kohm-pleh-tah-MEHN-teh ah-moo-eh-BLAH-doh

**I'm looking for an apartment with utilities included in the price**
*Estoy buscando un apartamento con servicios incluidos en el precio*
Ehs-TOH-ee boos-KAHN-doh oon ah-pahr-tah-MEHN-toh kohn sehr-VEE-see-ohs een-kloo-EE-dohs ehn ehl PREH-see-oh

**I am sorry but your card is not working**
*Lo siento, pero tu tarjeta no funciona*
Loh see-EHN-toh PEH-roh too tahr-HEH-tah noh foon-see-OH-nah

**You are spending too much money**
*Estás gastando demasiado dinero*
Ehs-TAHS gahs-THAN-doh deh-mah-see-AH-doh dee-NEH-roh

**I only have $20 dollars**
*Solo tengo $20 dólares*
SOh-loh TEHN-goh $20 DOH-lah-rehs

**Do you offer a payment plan?**
*¿Ofrece un plan de pagos?*
Oh-FREH-seh oon plahn deh PAH-gohs

**Do these two items come together?**
*¿Estas dos cosas vienen juntas?*
*EHS-tahs dohs KOH-sas vee-EH-nehn HOON-tahs*

**Where was this made?**
*¿Dónde se ha fabricado?*
*DOHN-deh seh ah fah-bree-KAH-doh*

**How much did you pay for that? That's a bargain!**
*¿Cuánto pagaste por eso? ¡Es una ganga!*
KWAHN-toh pah-GAHS-teh pohr EH-soh ehs OO-nah GAHN-gah

**Do you have a cheaper version of this item?**
*¿Tienes una versión más barata de este producto?*
Tee-EH-nehs OO-nah vehr-see-OHN mahs bah-RAH-tah deh EHS-teh proh-DOOK-toh

**I'll call you when I need you**
*Te llamaré cuando te necesite*
Teh yah-mah-REH KWAHN-doh teh neh-seh-SEE-teh

**Does this item have a warranty?**
*¿Este artículo tiene garantía?*
*EHS-teh ahr-TEE-koo-loh tee-EH-neh gah-rahn-TEE-ah*

**Do you accept returns?**
*¿ Aceptas devoluciones?*
Ah-sehp-TAHS- deh-voh-loo-see-OH-nehs

**I'm just looking, thank you**
*Solo estoy mirando, gracias*
SOH-loh ehs-TOH-ee mee-RAHN-doh GRAH-see-ahs

**Where is the changing room?**
*¿Dónde está el probador?*
DOHN-deh ehs-TAH ehl pro-bah-DOHR

**Where can I try this on?**
*¿Dónde puedo probarme esto?*
DOHN-deh PWEH-doh proh-BAHR-meh EHS-toh

**Where can I buy some souvenirs?**
*¿Dónde puedo comprar algunos souvenirs?*
DOHN-deh PWEH-doh kohm-PRAHR ahl-GOO-nohs soo-veh-NEERS

**Where is your ladies' section?**
*¿Dónde está la sección de mujeres?*
DOHN-deh ehs-TAH lah sek-see-OHN deh moo-HEH-rehs

**Where is your men's section?**
*¿Dónde está la sección de hombres?*
DOHN-deh ehs-TAH lah sek-see-OHN deh OHM-brehs

**Is there an ATM machine near-by?**
*¿Hay un cajero automático cerca?*
AH-ee oon kah-HEH-roh  ah-oo-toh-MAH-tee-koh SEHR-kah

**Do you take American dollars?**
*¿ Aceptas dólares americanos?*
Ah-sehp-TAHs- DOH-lah-rehs ah-meh-ree-KAH-nohs

**Do you take cash?**
*¿ Aceptas dinero en efectivo?*
Ah-sehp-TAHS- dee-NEH-roh ehn eh-fehk-TEE-voh

**Do you take credit card?**
*¿ Aceptas tarjetas de crédito?*
Ah-sehp-TAHS- tahr-HEH-tahs deh KREH-dee-toh

**I don't want anything, thanks**
*No quiero nada, gracias*
noh kee-EH-roh NAH-dah GRAH-see-ahs

**You owe me money**
*Me debes dinero*
Meh DEH-behs dee-NEH-roh

**Do you have change?**
*¿ Tienes cambio?*
Teeh- enehs KAHM-bee-oh

**I don't like it, but thank you.**
*No me gusta, pero gracias.*
Noh meh GOOS-tah PEH-roh GRAH-seeh-ahs

**What is the exchange rate right now?**
*¿Cuál es el tipo de cambio en este momento?*
KWAHL ehs ehl TEE-poh deh KAHM-bee-oh ehn EHS-teh moh-MEHN-toh

**Sorry, I'm not interested**
*Lo siento, no estoy interesada (femanine)*
Loh see-EHN-toh noh ehs-TOH-ee een-teh-reh-SAH-dah

**Sorry, I'm not interested**
*Lo siento, no estoy interesado (masculine)*
Loh see-EHN-toh noh ehs-TOH-ee een-teh-reh-SAH-dah

**Sorry, but I don't want it**
*Lo siento, pero no lo quiero*
Loh see-EHN-toh PEH-roh noh loh kee-EH-roh

**Where is the nearest place I can exchange money?**
*¿Dónde está el sitio más cercano para cambiar dinero?*
DOHN-deh ehs-TAH ehl SEE-tee-oh mahs sehr-KAH-noh PAH-rah kahm-bee-AHR dee-NEH-roh

### I would like a receipt please
*Quisiera un recibo, por favor*
Kee-see-EH-rah oon reh-SEE-boh pohr-fah-VOHR

### Yes, I will take it
Sí, me lo llevo
See meh loh YEH-voh

### I'll only take it if you drop the price by half
*Me lo llevaré solo si bajas el precio a la mitad*
Meh loh yeh-vah-REH SOH-loh see BAH-hahs ehl PREH-see-oh ah lah mee-TAHD

### That's a great price, I'll take it
*Es un gran precio, lo acepto*
Ehs oon grahn PREH-see-oh loh ah-SE-HP-toh

### Do you sell any souvenirs for tourists?
*¿Vendes algún recuerdo para turistas?*
VEHN-dehs ahl-GOON reh-kooh-EHR-doh PAH-rah too-REHS-tahs

### Are you able to ship these products overseas?
*¿Son capaces de enviar estos productos al extranjero?*
Sohn kah-PAH-sehs deh ehn-vee-AHR EHS-tohs proh-DOOK-tohs ahl ehks-trahn-HEH-roh

### Can I have a bag with that?
*¿Puede darme una bolsa por favor?*
PWEH-deh DAHR-meh OO-nah BOHL-sah pohr fah-VOHR

### We are closed, you can come tomorrow
*Estamos cerrados, puedes venir mañana*
Ehs-TAH-mohs seh-RRAH-dohs poo-EH-dehs veh-NEER mah-NYAH-nah

### No bag, I have my own
*No quiero bolsa, tengo la mía*
Noh kee-EH-roh BOHL-sah TEHN-goh lah MEE-ah

### Can I borrow some money?
*¿Me prestas algo de dinero?*
Meh PREHS-tahs AHL-goh deh dee-NEH-roh

### Is there any second-hand shop?
*¿Hay alguna tienda de segunda mano?*
AH-ee ahl-GOO-nah tee-EHN-dah deh seh-GOON-dah MAH-noh

### Is there any craft shop?
*¿Hay alguna tienda de artesanías?*
AH-ee ahl-GOO-nah tee-EHN-dah deh ahr-teh-sah-NEE-ahs

### What are you buying?
*¿Qué estás comprando?*
Keh ehs-TAHS kohm-PRAHN-doh

# Fashion and Clothes

### I ordered a leather jacket from this shop
*Pedí una chaqueta de cuero de esta tienda*
Peh-DEE OO-na chah-KEH-tah deh koo-EH-roh ehn EHS-tah tee-EHN-dah

### Did you see the cardigans in that advertisement?
*¿Viste rebecas  del anuncio?*
VEES-teh lohs reh-BEH-kahs dehl ah-NOON-see-oh

### I can't believe that we have the same dress
*No puedo creer que tengamos el mismo vestido*
Noh PWEH-doh kreh-EHR keh tehn-GAH-mohs ehl MEES-moh vehs-TEE-doh

### Where did you buy those shoes?
*¿Dónde  has comprado esos zapatos?*
DOHN-deh  ahs kohm-PRAH-doh EH-sohs sah-PAH-tohs

### I need a new coat
*Necesito un abrigo nuevo*
Neh-seh-see-toh oon ah-BREE-goh noo-EH-voh

### My hat is so old
*Mi sombrero es muy viejo*
Mee sohm-BREH-roh ehs MOO-ee vee-EH-hoh

### Your socks have holes
*Tus calcetines tienen agujeros*
Toos kahl-seh-TEE-nehs tee-EH-nehn ah-goo-HEH-rohs

### That jumper is very ugly
*Ese jersey es muy feo*
EH-seh hehr-SEH-ee ehs MOO-ee FEH-oh

### That style is quite old fashion
*Ese estilo  es anticuado*
EH-seh ehs-TEE-loh ehs ahn-tee-koo-AH-doh

### I will wear my new costume to the party
*Voy a llevar mi nuevo disfraz a la fiesta*
VOH-ee ah yeh-VAHR mee noo-EH-voh dees-FRAHZ ah lah fee-EHS-tah

### I feel motivated with these new gym clothes
*Me siento motivada con mi nueva ropa  de gimnasia*
Meh see-EHN-toh moh-tee-VAH-dah kohn mee noo-EH-vah ROH-pah  deh heem-NAH-see- ah

### My high heels broke during the party
*Mis tacones se rompieron du-rante la fiesta*
Mees tah-KOH-nehs seh rohm-pee-EH-rohn doo-RAHN-teh lah fee-EHS-tah

### I need a new jumpsuit for my job
*Necesito un mono nuevo para mi trabajo*
Neh-seh-SEE-toh oon MOH-noh noo-EH-voh PAH-rah mee trah-BAH-hoh

### You have to buy a swimsuit for this holiday
*Tienes que comprarte un traje de baño nuevo para estas vacaciones*
Tee-EH-nehs keh kohm-PRAHR-teh oon TRA he deh BA nee oh noo-EH-voh PAH-rah lahs vah-kah-see-OH-nehs

### He is wearing the ring that I bought for him
*Él lleva el anillo que le regalé*
Ehl YEH-vah ehl ah-NEE-yoh keh leh reh-gah-LEH

### It fits perfectly
*Me queda perfecto*
Meh KEH-dah pehr-FEHK-toh

### Do you ever buy beauty products?
*¿Alguna vez has comprado productos de belleza?*
Ahl-GOO-nah vehs ahs kohm-PRAH-doh proh-DOOK-tohs deh beh-YEH-sah

### Are these shirts for the new uniform?
*¿Estas camisas son para el uniforme nuevo?*
EHS-tahs kah-MEE-sahs sohn PAH-rah ehl oo-nee-FOHR-meh noo-EH-voh

### My jeans got smaller
*Mis vaqueros han encogido*
Mees vah-KEH-rohs ahn en –ko – HEE - doh

### I love the drawing in your t-shirt
*Me encanta el dibujo de tu camiseta*
Meh ehn-KAHN-tah ehl dee-BOO-hoh deh too kah-mee-SEH-tah

### This belt is too long
*Este cinturón es demasiado largo*
EHS-teh seen-too-ROHN ehs deh-mah-see-AH-doh LAHR-goh

### The blouse looks small on me
*La blusa me queda pequeña*
Lah BLOO-sah meh KEH-dah peh-KEH-nyah

### We bought a new pair of boots
*Hemos comprado un nuevo par de botas*
EH-mohs kohm-PRAH-doh oon noo-EH-voh pahr deh BOH-tahs

### Are you using the necklace tonight?
*¿Vas a usar el collar esta noche?*
Vahs ah oo-SAHR ehl koh-YAHR EHS-tah NOH-cheh

### I have a huge stain in my shirt
*Tengo una enorme mancha en mi camisa*
TEHN-goh OO-nah eh-NOHR-meh MAHN-chah ehn mee kah MEE sah

### Who is the designer of these outfits?
*¿Quién es el diseñador de estos conjuntos?*
Kee-EHN ehs ehl dee-seh-nyah-DOHR deh EHS-tohs kohn-HOOHN-tohs

### I love fashion
*Me encanta la moda*
Meh ehn-KAHN-tah lah MOH-dah

**Do you know how to sew your clothes?**
*¿Sabes cómo coser tu ropa?*
SAH-behs KOH-moh koh-SEHR too ROH-pah

**I like this combination**
*Me gusta esta combinación*
Meh GOOS-tah EHS-tah kohm-bee-nah-see-OHN

**Where is the accessories section?**
*¿Dónde está la sección de accesorios?*
DOHN-deh ehs-TAH lah sek-see-OHN deh ahk-seh-SOH-ree-ohs

**You should buy her a nice bracelet**
*Deberías comprarle una pulsera bonita*
Deh-beh-REE-ahs kohm-PRAHR-leh OO-nah pool-SEH-rah boh-NEE-tah

That lingerie is elegant
*Esa lencería es elegante*
EH-sah lehn-seh-REE-ah ehs eh-leh-GAHN-teh

**Those trousers look nice on you**
*Te quedan bien esos pantalones*
Teh KEH-dahn bee-EHN EH-sohs pahn-tah-LOH-nehs

**Are you selling extra-large sizes?**
*¿Vendes tallas extra largas?*
VEHN-dehs TAH-yahs EKS-trah LAHR-gahs

**They are too big for me**
*Son demasiado grandes para mi*
Sohn deh-mah-see-AH-doh GRAHN-dehs PAH-rah mee

**They are too small for me**
*Son demasiado pequeños para mi*
Sohn deh-mah-see-AH-doh peh-KEH-nyohs PAH-rah mee

**Can you show me...?**
*¿Puedes enseñarme...?*
PWEH-dehs ehn-seh-NYAHR-meh

**Do you have a smaller size?**
*¿Tienes una talla más pequeña?*
Tee-EH-nehs OO-nah TAH-yah mahs peh-KEH-nyah

**Do you have a bigger size?**
*¿Tienes una talla más grande?*
Tee-EH-nehs OO-nah TAH-yah mahs GRAHN-deh

# Colors and Patterns

**My favourite color is yellow**
*Mi color favorito es el amarillo*
Mee koh-LOHR fah-voh-REE-toh ehs el
ah-mah-REE-yoh

**Purple**
*Morado*
Moh-RAH-doh

**Red**
*Rojo*
ROH-hoh

**Black**
*Negro*
NEH-groh

**Gray**
*Gris*
Grees

**Green**
*Verdc*
VEHR-deh

**White**
*Blanco*
BLAHN-koh

**Gold**
*Dorado*
doh – RAH  doh

**Silver**
*Plateado*
Plah-teh-AH-doh

**Pink**
*Rosado*
Roh-SAH-doh

**Orange**
*Anaranjado*
ah-nah-rahn-HAH-doh

**Brown**
*Marrón*
Mah-RROHN

**Blue**
*Azul*
Ah-ZOOL

**Dark green**
*Verde oscuro*
VEHR-deh ohs-KOO-roh

**Lilac**
*Lila*
LEE-lah

**What is the color of this?**
*¿Qué color es este?*
Keh koh-LOHR ehs EHS-teh

**I am colour-blind**
*Soy daltónico*
SOO ee dahl-TOH-nee-koh

**What is your favourite color?**
*¿Cuál es tu color favorito?*
KWAHL ehs too coh-LOHR fah-voh-
REE-toh

55

**What color is…?**
*¿De qué color es…?*
Deh keh coh-LOHR ehs

**What is your favourite pattern?**
*¿Cuál es tu estampado favorito?*
KWAHL ehs too ehs-tahm-PAH-doh fah-voh-REE-toh

**I want dotted curtains**
*Quiero cortinas  tejidas*
Kee-EH-roh kohr-TEE-nahs  teh-HEE-dahs

**They have bought a stripped rug**
*Han comprado una alfombra a rayas*
Ahn kohm-PRAH-doh OO-nah ahl-FOHM-brah  ah RAH-yahs

**I have bought a plaid tie**
*o He comprado una corbata a cuadros*
eh kohm-PRAH-doh OO-nah kohr-BAH-tah  ah koo-AH-drohs

# Family

**This is my wife**
*Esta es mi esposa*
EHS-tah ehs mee ehs-POH-sah

**This is my husband**
*Este es mi marido*
EHS-teh ehs mee mah-REE-doh

**He is my brother**
# Él es mi hermano
Ehl ehs mee ehr-MAH-noh

**She is my sister**
*Ella es mi hermana*
EH-yah ehs mee ehr-MAH-nah

**These are our children**
*Estos son nuestros niños*
EHS-tohs sohn noo-EHS-trohs NEE-nyos

**I have not children**
*No tengo niños*
Noh TEHN-goh NEE-nyos

**This is my mother**
*Esta es mi madre*
EHS-tah ehs mee MAH-dreh

**This is my grandmother**
*Esta es mi abuela*
EHS-tah ehs mee ah-boo-EH-lah

**This is my father**
Este es mi padre
EHS-teh ehs mee PAH-dreh

**This is my grandfather**
*Este es mi abuelo*
EHS-teh ehs mee ah-boo-EH-loh

**He is my son-in-law**
*Él es mi yerno*
Ehl ehs mee YEHR-noh

**She is my daughter-in-law**
*Ella es mi nuera*
EH-yah ehs mee noo-EH-rah

**Have you met your mother-in-law?**
*¿Has conocido a tu suegra?*
Ahs koh-noh-SEE-doh ah too soo-EH-grah

**And your father-in-law?**
*¿Y a tu suegro?*
Ee ah too soo-EH-groh

**What is the age difference between you and your brother?**
*¿Cuál es la diferencia de edad entre tu y tu hermano?*
KWAHL ehs lah dee-feh-REHN-see-ah deh eh-DAHD EHN-treh too ee too ehr-MAH-noh

**Do you have brothers or sisters?**
*¿Tienes hermanos o hermanas?*
Teeh-EH-nehs ehr-MAH-nohs oh ehr-MAH-nahs

**How is your family?**
*¿Cómo está tu familia?*
KOH-moh ehs-TAH too fah-MEE-lee-ah

**The dog is our family pet**
*El perro es la mascota de la familia*
Ehl PEH-rroh ehs lah mahs-KOH-tah deh lah fah-MEE-lee-ah

**Where does your uncle live?**
*¿Dónde vive tu tío?*
DOHN-deh VEE-veh too TEE-oh

**Is he your cousin?**
*¿Es él tu primo?*
Ehs el too PREE-moh

**How old is your brother?**
*¿Cuántos años tiene tu hermano?*
KWAHN-tohs AH-nyos tee-EH-neh too ehr-MAH-noh

**How old is your sister?**
*¿Cuántos años tiene tu hermana?*
KWAHN-tohs AH-nyos tee-EH-neh too ehr-MAH-nah

**Was your family born here?**
*¿Tu familia nació aquí?*
Too fah-MEH-lee-ah ehs deh ah-KEE

**Are you married?**
*¿ Están casados?*
Ehs- TAN Kah-SAH-dohs

**I don't live with my family**
*No vivo con mi familia*
Noh VEE-voh kohn mee fah-MEE-lee-ah

**I live alone**
*Vivo solo*
VEE-voh SOH-loh

**My aunt and her children are coming for dinner tonight**
*Mi tia y sus hijos vienen a cenar esta noche*
Mee TEE-ah ee soos ee-HOHS vee-EH-nehn ah seh-NAHR EHS-tah NOH-cheh

**When did he die?**
*¿Cuándo ha muerto?*
KWAHN-doh ah moo-HER-toh

## Responses

**Family is everything**
*La familia es todo*
Lah fah-MEE-lee-ah chs TOH doh

**I am sorry for your loss**
*Siento mucho tu pérdida*
See-EHN-toh MOO-choh too PEHR-dee-dah

**I am here for a relative's wedding**
*Estoy aquí por la boda de un familiar*
Ehs-TOH-ee a-KEE pohr lah BOH-dah deh oon fah-mee-lee-AHR

**I have 1 sister**
*Tengo una hermana*
TEHN-goh OO-nah ehr-MAH-nah

**You were born with a silver spoon!**
*¡Has nacido con un pan bajo el brazo!*
Ahs nah-SEE-doh kohn oon pahn BAH-hoh ehl BRAH-soh

**I have 2 brothers**
*Tengo dos hermanos*
TEHN-goh dohs ehr-MAH-nohs

**I have 3 children**
*Tengo tres niños*
TEHN-goh trehs NEE-nyos

**My brother is 25 years old**
*Mi hermano tiene 25 años*
**Mee** ehr-MAH-noh tee-EH-neh 25 AH-nyos

**My sister is 40 years old**
*Mi hermana tiene 40 años*
**Mee** ehr-MAH-nah tee-EH-neh 40 AH-nyos

**My nephew is taller than me**
*Mi sobrino es más alto que yo*
Mee soh-BREE-noh ehs mahs AHL-toh keh yoh

**I am the eldest sibling**
*Soy el hermano mayor*
SOH-ee ehl ehr-MAH-noh mah-YOHR

**I am the youngest sibling**
*Soy el hermano menor*
SOH-ee ehl ehr-MAH-noh meh-NOHR

**My parents are divorced**
*Mis padres están divorciados*
Mees PAH-drehs ehs-TAHN dee-vohr-see-AH-dohs

**I am adopted**
*Soy adoptado*
SOH-ee ah-dohp-TAH-doh

**I am an orphan**
*Soy huérfano*
SOH-ee oo-EHR-fah-noh

**I don't have siblings**
*No tengo hermanos*
Noh TEHN-goh ehr-MAH-nohs

**Yes, my family is from here**
*Sí, mi familia es de aquí*
See meh fah-MEE-lee-ah ehs deh ah-KEE

**No, I am not married**
*No, no estoy casada*
Noh noh ehs-TOH-ee kah-SAH-dah

**My niece is smaller than me**
*Mi sobrina es más pequeña que yo*
Mee soh-BREE-nah ehs mahs peh-KEH-nyah keh yoh

# Celebrations

## Happy birthday!
*¡Feliz cumpleaños!*
Feh-LEES koom-pleh-AH-nyos

## Today is a special day!
*¡Hoy es un día especial!*
OH-ee ehs oon DEE-ah ehs-peh-see-AHL

## Congratulations!
*Felicitaciones*
feh – lee – see – tah –ZEEO – nehs

## Have fun!
*Diviértete!*
Dee-vee-EHR-teh-teh

## Have a good birthday!
*¡Que tengas un buen cumpleaños!*
Keh TEHN-gahs oon BWEHN coom-pleh-AH-nyos

## Have a special day!
*¡Que tengas un día especial!*
Keh TEHN-gahs oon DEE-ah ehs-peh-see-AHL

## Hope that you have many birthdays!
*¡Espero que tengas muchos cumpleaños!*
**Ehs-PEH-reoh keh** TEHN-gahs MOO-chohs coom-pleh-AH-nyos

## Blow the candles!
*¡Sopla las velas!*
SOH-plah lahs VEH-lahs

## It will give you luck
*Te dará suerte*
The dah-RAH soo-HER-teh

## Hope all your dreams come true!
*¡Espero que todos tus sueños se hagan realidad!*
Ehs-PEH-roh keh TOH-dohs toos SWEH-nyos seh AH-gahn reh-ah-lee-DAHD

## It is a miracle!
*¡Es un milagro!*
Ehs oon mee-LAH-groh

## Best wishes!
*¡Mis mejores deseos!*
Meehs meh-HOH-rehs deh-SEH-ohs

## Congratulations on getting engaged!
*¡Felicidades por el compromiso!*
Feh-lee-see-DAH-dehs pohr ehl kohm-proh-MEE-soh

## Congratulations on your marriage!
*¡Felicidades por tu matrimonio!*
Feh-lee-see-DAH-dehs pohr too mah-treh-MOH-nee-oh

## Congratulations on your newborn!
*¡Felicidades por tu recién nacido!*
Feh-lee-see-DAH-dehs pohr too reh-see-EHN na-SEE-doh

## I am very happy! Is it a boy or a girl?
*¡Estoy muy feliz! ¿Es un niño o una niña?*
Ehs-TOH-ee MOO-eh feh-LEES ehs oon NEE-nyo oh OO-nah NEE-nya

## When is your birthday?
*¿Cuándo es tu cumpleaños?*
KWAHN-doh ehs too koom-pleh-AH-nyos

## How old are you today?
*¿Cuántos años cumples hoy?*
KWAHN-tohs AH-nyos KOOM-plehs OH-ee

## What do you want for your birthday?
*¿Qué quieres por tu cumpleaños?*
Keh kee-EH-rehs pohr too kohm-ple-AH-nee-ohs

## What are you going to do for your birthday?
*¿Qué vas a hacer por tu cumpleaños?*
Keh vahs ah ah-CEHR pohr too koom-ple-AH-nyos

## Happy New Year!
*¡Feliz año nuevo!*
Feh-LEES AH-nyoh noo-EH-voh

## Happy Christmas!
*¡Feliz Navidad!*
Feh-LEES nah-vee-DAHD

## It's carnival!
*¡Es carnaval!*
Ehs kahr-nah-VAHL

## Here is your gift, I hope that you enjoy it!
*Aquí tienes tu regalo, ¡Espero que lo disfrutes!*
Ah-KEE tee-EH-nehs too reh-GAH-loh ehs-PEH-roh keh loh dees-FROO-tehs

## Who's birthday is it?
*¿De quién es el cumpleaños?*
Deh kee-EHN ehs ehl koom-ple-AH-nyos

## Is this a religious celebration?
*¿Es esta una celebración religiosa?*
Ehs EHS-tah OO-nah seh-leh-brah-see-OHN reh-lee-gee-OH-sah

## When is holy week?
*¿Cuándo es Semana Santa?*
KWAHN-doh ehs seh-MAH-nah SAHN-tah

## I don't like this present
*No me gusta este regalo*
Noh meh GOOS-tah EHS-teh reh-GAH-loh

## I wasn't expecting this present
*No esperaba este regalo*
Noh ehs-peh-RAH-bah EHS-teh reh-GAH-loh

## You will like it
*Te gustará*
Teh goos-tah-RAH

**I bought you a gift**
*Te he comprado un regalo*
Teh eh kohm-PRAH-doh oon reh-GAH-loh

**We should throw a party!**
*¡Deberíamos hacer una fiesta!*
Deh-beh-REE-ah-mohs ah-SEHR OO-nah fee-EHS-tah

# Common Questions

**Do you speak english?**
*¿Hablas inglés?*
AH-blahs een-GLEHS

**How do you say this in Spanish?**
*¿Cómo se dice esto en español?*
KOH-moh seh DEE-seh EHS-toh ehn ehs-pah-NYOHL

**Where is the bathroom?**
*¿Dónde está el baño?*
DOHN-deh ehs-TAH ehl BAH-nyoh

**Could you repeat that?**
*¿Podrías repetir eso?*
Poh-DREE-ahs reh-peh-TEER EH-soh

**Could you speak slower?**
*¿Podrías hablar más lento?*
Poh-DREE-ahs ah-BLAHR mahs – LEN-toh

**Write it down please**
*Escríbelo por favor*
Ehs-CREE-beh-loh pohr fah-VOHR

**How do you say this word?**
*¿Cómo se dice esta palabra?*
KOH-moh seh DEE-seh EHS-tah pah-LAH-brah

**It was a misunderstanding**
*Era un malentendido*
EH-rah oon mahl-ehn-tehn-DEE-doh

**What's the best thing that happened to you this year?**
*¿Qué es lo mejor que te ha pasado en este año?*
Keh ehs loh meh-HOHR keh teh ah pah-SAH-doh ehn EHS-teh AH-nyoh

**Where did you grow up?**
*¿Dónde te has criado?*
DOHN-deh teh ahs kree – AH - doh

**What do you do for fun?**
*¿Qué haces para divertirte?*
Keh AH-sehs PAH-rah dee-vehr-TEER-teh

**Are you a starbucks fan?**
*¿Eres fan de Starbucks?*
EH-rehs fahn deh STAHR-bucks

**What sort of music do you like?**
*¿Qué tipo de música te gusta?*
Keh TEE-poh deh MOO-seh-kah teh GOOS-tah

**Do you like sports?**
*¿Te gustan los deportes?*
Teh GOOS-tahn lohs deh-POHR-tehs

**Do you study here?**
*¿Estudias aquí?*
Ehs-TOO-dee-ahs ah-KEE

**How do you know the host?**
*¿De dónde conoces al anfitrión?*
deh DON – deh koh-NOH-sehs ahl ahn-fee-tree-OHN

**Can you help me?**
*¿Puedes ayudarme?*
PWEH-dehs ah-yoo-DAHR-meh

**Where do you live?**
*¿Dónde vives?*
DOHN-deh VEE-vehs

**What does that mean?**
*¿Qué significa eso?*
Keh seeg-neh-FEE-kah EH-soh

**Can I ask you a question?**
*¿Puedo hacerte una pregunta?*
PWEH-doh ah-SEHR-teh OO-nah preh-GOON-tah

**Are you religious?**
*¿Eres religioso?*
EH-rehs reh-lee-hee-OH-soh

**Do you understand?**
*¿Entiendes?*
ehn-tee-EHN-dehs

**What's the time?**
*¿Qué hora es?*
Keh OH-rah ehs

**What's the weather like today?**
*¿ ¿Cómo está el clima hoy?*
KOH moh - es TAH - el - KLEE mah - ohee

**Where can I buy…?**
*¿Dónde puedo comprar…?*
DOHN-deh PWEH-doh kohm-PR

**Write that information down on this piece of paper please**
*Escribe esa información en este papel por favor*
Ehs-KREE-beh EH-sah een-fohr-mah-see-OHN ehn EHS-teh pah-PEHL por fah vor

**Are you saving money?**
*¿Estás ahorrando dinero?*
Ehs-TAHS ah-oh-RRAHN-doh dee-NEH-roh

**What do you need?**
*¿Qué necesitas?*
Keh neh-seh-SEE-tahs

**Whose is this phone?**
*¿De quién es este móvil?*
Deh kee-EHN ehs EHS-teh MOH-veel

**Who is there?**
*¿Quién está allí?*
Kee-EHN ehs-TAH ah-YEE

**What is in the box?**
*¿Qué hay en la caja?*
Keh AH-ee ehn lah KAH-hah

**Can you pick me up?**
*¿Puedes recogerme?*
PWEH-dehs reh-koh-HEHR-meh

# Responses

## I can't understand you
*No te entiendo*
Noh teh ehn-tee-EHN-doh

## I can understand you
*Te puedo entender*
Teh PWEH-doh ehn-tehn-DEHR

## I like any music genre
*Me gusta cualquier género musical*
Meh GOOS-tah koo-ahl-kee-EHR HEH-neh-roh moo-seh-KAHL

## Someone is calling me
*Alguien me está llamando*
AHL-gee-ehn meh ehs-TAH yah-MAHN-doh

## What do you want to show me?
*¿Qué quieres enseñarme?*
Keh kee-EH-rehs ehn-seh-NYAHR-meh

## Your phone is ringing
*Tu teléfono está sonando*
Too teh-LEH-foh-noh ehs-TAH soh-NAHN-doh

## That means that…
*Eso significa que…*
EH-soh seeg-nee-FEE-kah keh

## I haven't saved any money
*No he ahorrado nada*
Noh eh ah-oh-RRAH-doh NAH-dah

## I have all my money in a money box
*Tengo todo mi dinero en una alcancía*
TEHN-goh TOH-doh mee dee-NEH-roh ehn OO-nah   al kan SHEE ah

## Yes
*Sí*
see

## No
*No*
Noh

## Maybe
*Quizás*
Kee-SAHS

## Never
*Nunca*
NOON-kah

## Hardly ever
*Casi nunca*
KAH-see NOON-kah

## Sometimes
*A veces*
Ah VEH-sehs

## Mostly
*Casi siempre*
KAH-see see-EHM-preh

## It is mine
*Es mío*
Ehs MEE-oh

## It is yours
*Es tuyo*
Ehs TOO-yoh

## I am on holiday
*Estoy de vacaciones*
Ehs-TOO-ee deh vah-kah-see-OH-nehs

### I can't right now, I am on the phone
*No puedo ahora mismo, estoy hablando por teléfono*
Noh PWEH-doh ah-OH-rah MEES-moh ehs-TOH-ee ah-BLAHN-doh pohr teh-LEH-foh-noh

### He is making a call
*Está haciendo una llamada*
Ehs-TAH ah-see-EHN-doh OO-nah yah-MAH-dah

### I just woke up
*Me acabo de despertar*
Meh ah-KAH-boh deh dehs-pehr-TAHR

### I hate waking up early
*Odio levantarme temprano*
OH-dee-oh leh-vahn-TAHR-meh tehm-PRAH-noh

### I just moved here
*Acabo de mudarme aquí*
Ah-KAH-boh deh moo-DAHR-meh ah-KEE

### I am new here
*Soy nuevo aquí*
SOH-ee noo-EH-voh ah-KEE

### I am learning Spanish
*Estoy aprendiendo español*
Ehs-TOO-eh ah-prehn-dee-EHN-doh ehs-pah-NYOHL

### I love your country
*Me encanta tu país*
Meh ehn-KAHN-tah too pah-EEHS

### You have to disinfect your hands
*Tienes que desinfectarte las manos*
Tee-EH-nehs keh dehs-een-fehk-TAHR-teh lahs MAH-nohs

## Technology

### Where is the closest cafe with good Wi- Fi?
*¿Dónde está el café más cercano con buen Wi-Fi?*
DOHN-deh ehs-TAH ehl ka-FEH mahs sehr-KAH-noh kohn WEE-fee

### Do you have Wi-Fi here?
*¿Tienes Wi-Fi aquí?*
tee-EH-nehs WEE-fee SEHR-kah

### Is there an internet cafe closeby?
*¿Hay un cibercafé cerca?*
AH-ee oon SEE-behr kah-FEH SEHR-kah

### Do you have Facebook or Instagram?
*¿Tienes Facebook o Instagram?*
Tee-EH-nehs FEH-ees-book oh EENS-tah-grahm

**What is the Wi-Fi password?**
*¿Cuál es la contraseña del Wi-Fi?*
KWAHL ehs lah kohn-trah-SEH-nyah dehl WEE-fee

**The Wi-Fi seems to be slow, can you please check the problem?**
*El Wi-Fi parece ir lento, ¿ Puedes por favor comprobar el problema?*
Ehl WEE-fee pah-REH-seh eer LEHN-toh PWEH-dehs por favor kohm-proh-BAHR ehl proh-BLEH-mah

**The Wi-Fi does not seem to be working, can you please check?**
*El Wi-Fi no parece estar funcionando, ¿ Puedes comprobarlo?*
Ehl WEE-fee noh pah-REH-seh ehs-TAHR foon-see-oh NAHN-doh PWEH-dehs kohm-proh-BAHR-loh

**I'm having trouble getting online, can you please help?**
*Estoy teniendo problemas para conectarme, ¿ Puedes ayudarme?*
Ehs-TOO-ee teh-nee-EHN-doh proh-BLEH-mahs PAH-rah koh-nchk TAHR-meh PWEH-dehs ah-yoo-DAHR-meh

**Can I check the Wi-Fi speed before sitting down?**
*¿Puedo comprobar la velocidad del Wi-Fi antes de sentarme?*
PWEH-doh kohm-proh-BAHR lah veh-loh-see-DAHD dehl WE

**Do you have a power outlet so I can charge my phone?**
*¿Tienes un enchufe para que pueda cargar mi teléfono?*
Tee-EH-nehs oon ehn-CHOO-feh PAH-rah keh poo-EH-dah kahr-GAHR mee teh-LEH-foh-noh

**Do you have an iPhone charger I can use?**
*¿Tienes un cargador de iPhone que pueda usar?*
Tee-EH-nehs oon kahr-gah-DOHR deh AH-ee-fohn keh PWEH-dah oo-SAHR

**Do you have a cell phone charger I can use?**
*¿Tienes un cargador de móvil que pueda usar?*
Tee-EH-nehs oon kahr-gah-DOHR deh MOH-veel keh PWEH-dah oo-SAHR

**Do you have this type of charger for my laptop?**
*¿Tienes este tipo de cargador para mi portátil?*
Tee-EH-nehs EHS-teh TEE-poh deh kahr-gah-DOHR PAH-rah mee pohr-TAH-tcel

**What is the login information for this computer?**
*¿Cuál es la información de acceso para esta computadora?*
KWAHL ehs lah een-fohr-mah-see-OHN deh ahk-SEH-soh PAH-rah EHS-tah com-poo-tah-DOH-rah

**What is your Instagram handle?**
*¿Cuál es tu Instagram?*
KWAHL ehs too EENS-tah-grahm

**What do you charge for computer use?**
*¿Cuánto cobras por usar una computadora?*
KWAHN-toh KOH-brahs pohr oo-SAHR oona com-poo-tah-DOH-rah

**What is your name on Facebook?**
*¿Cuál es tu nombre en Facebook?*
KWAHL ehs too NOHM-breh ehn FEH-ees-book

**I don't understand anything about technology**
*No entiendo nada de tecnología*
Noh ehn-tee-EHN-doh NAH-dah deh tehk-noh-loh-HEE-ah

**This computer is very slow**
*Esta computadora es muy lenta*
EHS-tah com-poo-tah-DOH-rahehs MOO-ee LEHN-tah

**Is this the fastest computer here?**
*¿Es esta la computadora más rápida aquí?*
Ehs EHS-tah lah com-poo-tah-DOH-rah mahs RAH-pee-dah ah-KEE

**Where can I plug this in?**
*¿Dónde puedo conectar esto?*
DOHN-deh PWEH-doh koh-nehk-TAHR EHS-toh

**I need help pairing my bluetooth device.**
*Necesito ayuda para emparejar mi dispositivo bluetooth.*
neh-seh-SEE-toh ah-YOO-dah PAH-rah ehm-pah-reh-HAHR mee dees-poh-seh-TEE-voh BLOO-tooth

**I need a longer ethernet cable.**
*Necesito un cable Ethernet más largo*
neh-seh-SEE-toh oon KAH-bleh EH-thehr-neht mahs LAHR-goh

**I don't know how to use the computer**
*No sé cómo usar la computadora*
Noh seh KOH-moh oo-SAHR lha com-poo-tah-DOH-rah

**I need to buy a new computer**
*Necesito comprarme una computadora nueva*
neh-seh-SEE-toh kohm-PRAHR-meh oona com-poo-tah-DOH-rahnoo-EH-vah

**I have bought new headphones**
*He comprado auriculares nuevos*
Eh kohm-PRAH-doh ah-oo-ree-koo-LAH-rehs noo-EH-vohs

**How much do you pay for your phone contract?**
*¿Cuánto pagas por el contrato de tu teléfono?*
KWAHN-toh PAH-gahs pohr ehl cohn-TRAH-toh deh too teh-LEH-foh-noh

**Do you use Youtube?**
*¿Usas Youtube?*
OO-sahs yoh-oo-too-beh

### How many views does your profile have?
*¿Cuántas visitas tiene tu perfil?*
KWAHN-tahs vee-SEE-tahs tee-EH-neh too pehr-FEEL

### I have a Youtube channel
Tengo un canal de Youtube
TEHN-goh oon kah-NAHL deh yoh-oo-too-beh

### How many followers do you have?
*¿Cuántos seguidores tienes?*
KWAHN-tohs seh-gee-DOH-rehs tee-EH-nehs

### What is your favorite app?
*¿Cuál es tu aplicación favorita?*
KWAHL ehs too ah-plee-kah-see-OHN fah-voh-REE-tah

### Do you want to join the group chat?
*¿ Quieres unirte al chat del grupo?*
Kee-EH-rehs oo-NEER te ahl chaht del GROO-poh

### How many photos do you post per day?
*¿Cuántas fotos publicas al día?*
KWAHN-tahs FOH-tohs poo-BLEEH-kahs ahl DEE-ah

### I have requested you on Instagram
*Te he solicitado en Instagram*
Teh eh soh-lee-see-TAH-doh ehn EENS-tah-grahm

### Tag me in your post
*Etiquétame en tu publicacion*
Eh-tee-KEH-tah-meh ehn too poo-blee-kah-see-OHN

### You must report this account
*Debes denunciar esta cuenta*
DEH-behs reh-noon-see-AHR EHS-tah koo-EHN-tah

### You should block him
*Deberías bloquearlo*
Deh-beh-REE-ahs bloh-keh-AHR-loh

### I don't use social media
*No uso redes sociales*
Noh OO-soh REH-dehs soh-see-AH-lehs

### Send me an email
*Mándame un correo*
MAHN-dah-meh oon koh-RREH-oh

### Follow me
*Sígueme*
SEE-geh-meh

# The Weather

**What is the weather like tomorrow?**
*¿ Cómo estará el tiempo mañana?*
KOH moh es ta RAH el tee-EHM-poh
mah-NYAH-nah

**Do you know the temperature today?**
*¿Sabes la temperatura de hoy?*
SAH-behs lah tehm-peh-rah-TOO-rah deh
OH-ee

**Will it rain today?**
*¿Lloverá hoy?*
yoh-veh-RAH OH-ee

**What a beautiful day!**
*¡Qué día tan lindo!*
Keh DEE-ah tahn LEEN doh

**Will it rain tomorrow?**
*¿Lloverá mañana?*
yoh-veh-RAH ma-NYAH-nah

**We couldn't ask for a better weather**
No hemos podido tener mejor tiempo
Noh EH-mohs poh-DEE-doh teh-NEHR
meh-HOHR tee-EHM-poh

**It's hot today**
*Hoy hace calor*
OH-ee AH-seh kah-LOHR

**What is the average temperature in summer?**
*¿Cuál es la temperatura media en verano?*
KWAHL ehs lah tehm-peh-rah-TOO-rah
MEH-dee-ah ehn veh-RAH-noh

**What is the average temperature**
*¿Cuál es la temperatura media?*
KWAHL ehs lah tehm-peh-rah-TOO-rah
MEH-dee-ah

**What is the weather forecast?**
*¿Cuál es la previsión del tiempo?*
KWAHL ehs lah preh-vee-see-OHN dehl
tee-EHM-poh

**There is a storm coming**
*Se acerca una tormenta*
Seh ah-SEHR-kah OO-nah tohr-MEHN-tah

**It's cold today**
*Hoy hace frío*
OH-ee AH-seh FREE-oh

**It will be cold tomorrow**
*Mañana hará frío*
ma-NYAH-nah ah-RAH FREE-oh

**The sky is clear**
*El cielo está despejado*
Ehl see-EH-loh ehs-TAH dehs-peh-HAH-doh

**It will be hot tomorrow**
*Mañana hará calor*
ma-NYAH-nah ah-RAH kah-LOHR

**The weather here is very pleasant**
*El tiempo aquí es muy agradable*
EHL tee-EHM-poh ah-KEE ehs MOO-eh ah-grah-DAH-ble

**The weather here has been very miserable**
*El tiempo aquí ha sido horrible*
EHL tee-EHM-poh ah-KEE ah SEE-doh oh-RREE-bleh

**Does it rain a lot here?**
*¿Llueve mucho aquí?*
yoo-EH-veh MOO-choh ah-KEE

**I am roasting**
*Me muero de calor*
Meh moo-EH-roh deh kah-LOHR

**I am sweaty**
*Estoy sudando*
*Ehs-TOH-ee soo-DAHN-doh*

**It is sunny today**
*Está soleado hoy*
Ehs-TAH soh-leh-AH-doh OH ee

**It is raining today**
*Está lloviendo hoy*
Ehs-TAH yoh-vee-EHN-doh OH-ee

**A thunderstorm just passed**
*Ha pasado una tormenta*
ah pah-SAH-doh OO-nah tohr-MEHN-tah

**Is that a hurricane?**
*¿Eso es un huracán?*
EH-soh ehs oon oo-rah-KAHN

**The fog is intense at this time**
*La niebla es intensa a esta hora*
Lah nee-EH-blah ehs een-TEHN-sah ah EHS-tah OH-rah

**It is cloudy**
*Está nublado*
Ehs-TAH noh-BLAH-doh

**It is windy**
*Está ventoso*
Ehs-TAH ven-TOH-soh

**It is snowing**
*Está nevando*
Ehs-TAH neh-VAHN-doh

**Snowflakes are so pretty**
*Los copos de nieve son muy bonitos*
Lohs KOH-pohs deh nee-EH-veh sohn MOO-ee boh-NEE-tohs

**Such a small rainbow**
*Qué arcoíris tan pequeño*
Keh ahr-koh-EE rees tahn peh-KEH-nyoh

**There is a flood**
*Hay una inundación*
AH-ee OO-nah ee-noon-dah-see-OHN

**Did you feel the earthquake?**
*¿Sentiste el terremoto?*
Sehn-'TEES-teh ehl teh-rreh-MOH-toh

**I am scared of the lightning**
*Tengo miedo a los relámpagos*
TEHN-goh mee-EH-doh ah lohs reh-LAHM-pah-gohs

# Expressions

**Stop!**
*¡Para!*
PAH-rah

**Wait!**
*¡Espera!*
Ehs-PEH-rah

**Have fun!**
*¡Pásalo bien!*
PAH-sah-loh bee-EHN

**Bon appetit!**
*¡Qué aproveche!*
Keh ah-proh-VEH-cheh

**Well done!**
*¡Bien hecho!*
*Bee-EHN EH-choh*

**Cheers!**
*¡Salud!*
Sah-LOOD

**I like it**
*Me gusta*
Meh GOOS-tah

**You win some you lose some**
*Ganas unos y pierdes otros*
GAH-nahs OO-nohs ee pee-EHR-dehs
OH-trohs

**Nothing ventured, nothing gained**
*Quien no arriesga, no gana*
Kee-EHN noh ah-rree-EHS-gah noh
GAH-nah

**People get what they deserve**
*Las personas tienen lo que se merecen*
Lahs pehr-SOH-nah tee-EH-nehn loh keh
seh meh-REH-sehn

**He's every inch a man**
*Es todo un hombre*
Ehs TOH-doh oon OHM-breh

**A penny for your thoughts**
*Un centavo por sus pensamientos*
Oon sehn-TAH-voh pohr toos
pehn-sah-mee-EHN-tohs

**Hold your horses!**
*¡Para el carro!*
PAH-rah ehl KAH-rroh

**I can dream, can't I?**
Puedo soñar, ¿ No?
Poo-EH-doh soh-NYAHR noh

**It doesn't ring a bell**
*No me suena*
Noh meh soo-EH-nah

70

**I wouldn't touch it with a barge pole (or a 10 ft. pole)**
*No lo tocaría ni con un palo*
Noh loh toh-kah-REE-ah nee kohn oon PAH-loh

**I wouldn't dream of it!**
*¡Ni se me ocurriría!*
Nee seh meh oh-koo-rree-REE-ah

**I mean it**
*Lo digo en serio*
Loh DEE-goh ehn SEH-reeh-oh

**It's a stone's throw from here**
*A un tiro de piedra de aquí*
Ah oon TEE-roh deh pee-EH-drah deh ah-KEE

**It was a slip of the tongue**
*Fue un descuido*
FWEH oon dehs-KWEE-doh

**It's about time!**
*¡Es hora!*
Era OH - rah

**It's like looking for a needle in a haystack**
*Es como buscar una aguja en un pajar*
Ehs KOH-moh boos-KAHR OO-nah ah-GOO-hah ehn oon pah-HAHR

**It's none of your business!**
*¡No es asunto tuyo!*
Noh ehs ah-SOON-toh TOO-yoh

**It's not all fun and games**
*No todo es diversión y juegos*
Noh TOH-doh ehs dee-vehr-see-OHN ee hoo-EH-gohs

**It's raining cats and dogs**
*Llueve a cántaros*
Yoo-EH-veh ah KAHN-tah-rohs

**Speaking of the devil...**
*Hablando de Roma...*
Ah-BLAHN-doh deh ROH-mah

**That goes without saying**
*Ni hace falta decirlo*
nee AH-seh FAHL-tah deh-SEER-loh

**There's something fishy here**
*Aquí hay algo sospechoso*
Ah-KEE AH-ee AHL-goh sohs-peh-CHOH-soh

**You can't miss it**
*No puedes perdértelo*
Noh poo-EH-dehs pehr-DEHR-teh-loh

**Let's get this over with**
*Vamos a terminar con esto*
VAH-mohs ah tehr-mee-NAHR kohn EHS-toh

**You have to face the music**
*Tienes que dar la cara*
Tee-EH-nehs keh dahr lah KAH-rah

**The early bird catches the worm**
*Al que madruga, Dios le ayuda*
Ahl keh mah-DROO-gah dee-OHS leh ah-YOO-dah

**Full belly, happy heart**
*Panza llena, corazón contento*
PAN zah – YEH nah - koh rah SOHN – kon TEN toh

**When it rains, it pours**
*No hay dos sin tres*
noh AEE dos seen TRES

**Better late than never**
*Mejor tarde que nunca*
Meh-HOHR TAHR-deh keh NOON-kah

**Break a leg**
*Buena suerte*
Boo-EH-nah soo-EHR-teh

**Pull yourself together**
*Tranquilízate*
Trahn-kee-LEE-sah-teh

**It's not rocket science**
*No es complicado*
Noh ehs cohm-plee-KAH-doh

**Birds of a feather flock together**
*Dios los cría y ellos se juntan*
Dee-OHS lohs KREE-ah ee EH-yohs seh HOON-tahn

**Kill two birds with one stone**
*Matar dos pájaros de un tiro*
mah-TAHR dohs PAH-hah-rohs deh oon TEE-roh

**Never bite the hand that feeds you**
*Nunca muerdas la mano que te da de comer*
NOON-kah moo-EHR-dahs lah MAH-noh keh the dah deh koh-MEHR

**It takes one to know one**
*Cree el lardón que todos son de su condición*
KREH-eh ehl lah-DROHN keh TOH-dohs sohn deh soo kohn-dee-see-OHN

**Break the ice**
*Romper el hielo*
Rohm-PEHR ehl ee-EH-loh

**If your shoe fits, wear it**
*El que se pica, ajos come*
Ehl keh seh PEE-kah AH-hohs KOH-meh

**A known evil is better than an unknown good**
*Más vale malo conocido que bueno por conocer*
Mahs VAH-leh MAH-loh koh-noh-SEE-doh keh boo-EH-noh pohr koh-noh-SEHR

**The bad ones never die**
*Hierba mala nunca muere*
ee-HER-bah MAH-lah NOON-kah moo-EH-reh

**I'll believe it when I see it**
*Lo creeré cuando lo vea*
Loh kreh-eh-REH KWAHN-doh loh VEH-ah

**Getting up early doesn't make the sun rise sooner**
*No por mucho madrugar, se amanece más temprano*
Noh pohr MOO-choh mah-droo-GAHR seh ah-mah-NEH-she mahs them-PRAH-noh

**Don't put the cart before the horse**
*No empieces la casa por el tejado*
Noh ehm-pee-EH-sehs lah KAH-sah pohr ehl teh-HAH-doh

**It is like putting a drop into a bucket**
*Es como echarle agua al mar*
Ehs KOH-moh eh-CHAHR-leh AH-gwah ahl mahr

# Idioms

You are as crazy as a bat
*Estás más loco que una cabra*
Ehs-TAHS mahs LOH-koh keh OO-nah
KAH-brah

You are nobody
*Eres un don nadie*
EH-rehs oon dohn NAH-dee-eh

I feel like I am worthless
*Siento que soy un cero a la izquierda*
See-EHN-toh keh SOH-ee oon SHE-roh
ah lah ees-kee-ER-dah

I was thrown under the bus
*Fui carne de cañón*
Foo-EE KAHR-neh deh kah-NYOHN

Does the school have a long holiday?
*¿El colegio hace puente?*
Ehl koh-LEH-hee-oh AH-she poo-EHN-the

We were very few people in the party
*Fuimos cuatro gatos locos en la fiesta*
Foo-EE-mohs koo-AH-troh GAH-tohs
LOH kos ehn lah fee-EHS-tah

You should talk to your teacher just in case
*Deberías hablar con tu profesora por las dudas*
Deh-beh-REE-ahs ah-BLAHR kohn too
proh-feh-SOH-rah pohr lahs DOO dahs

We have such a bad luck
*Que lo parió*
KEH loh pa REEO

I have come out of the closet
*He salido del armario*
Eh sah-LEE-doh dehl ahr-MAH-ree-oh

You scratch my back I'll scratch yours
*Hoy por ti, mañana por mi*
OH-ee pohr tee manNYAH-nah pohr mee

He / She goes off the rails
*Es la oveja negra*
Ehs lah oh-VEH-hah NEH-grah

You are blind as a bat
*Eres ciego como un vampíro*
Eres CEE-ego koh moh oon vam-PEE-roh

You have to look at the bright side
*Al mal tiempo, buena cara*
Ahl mahl tee-EHM-poh boo-EH-nah
KAH-rah

**The man tricked me**
*El hombre me dio gato por liebre*
Ehl OHM-breh meh dee-OH GAH-toh pohr lii-EH-breh

**You are excessively optimist**
*Lo ves todo de color de rosa*
Loh vehs TOH-doh deh koh-LOHR deh ROH-sah

**They have eaten loke horses**
*Se han puesto morados*
She ahn poo-EHS-toh moh-RAH-dohs

**They called you every name on the book**
*Te pusieron verde*
The poo-see-EH-rohn VEHR-deh

**Do you belong to the royalty?**
*¿Tienes sangre azul?*
Tee-EH-nehs SAHN-greh ah-SOOL

**He always turns the tables**
*Siempre le da la vuelta a la tortilla*
See-EHM-preh leh dah lah voo-EHL-tah ah lah tohr-TEE-yah

**Thank God you saw the writing on the wall**
*Gracias a Dios le viste las orejas al lobo*
GRAH-see-ahs ah dee-OHS leh VEES-the lahs oh-REH-hahs ahl LOH-boh

**I haven't found my better half yet**
*No he encontrado mi media naranja todavía*
Noh eh ehn-kohn-TRAH-doh mee MEH-dee-ah nah-RAHN-hah toh-dah-VEE-ah

**You have a memory like a sieve**
*Tienes memoria de pez*
Tee-EH-nehs meh-MOH-ree-ah deh pehs

**That is a piece of cake**
*Eso es pan comido*
EH-soh ehs pahn koh-MEE-doh

**She gave me the brush off**
*Ella me dio calabazas*
EH-yah meh dee-OH kah-lah-BAH-sahs

**They talk without mincing words**
*Ellos hablan sin pelos en la lengua*
EH-yohs AH-blahn seen PEH-lohs ehn lah LEHN-goo-ah

**Before the concert, you were like a cat in hot bricks**
*Antes del concierto, estabas como un flan*
AHN-tehs dehl kohn-see-HER-toh ehs-TAH-bahs KOH-moh oon flahn

**We are sick to death of this**
*Estamos hasta las narices de esto*
Ehs-TAH-mohs AHS-tah lahs nah-REE-sehs deh EHS-toh

**You got me in a bad mood**
*Me has puesto de mala leche*
Meh ahs poo-EHS-toh deh MAH-lah LEH-cheh

**I am a night owl**
*Soy un ave nocturna*
SOH-ee oon AH-veh nohk-TOOR-nah

**That is impossible to find**
*Es como buscar una aguja en un pajar*
Ehs KOH-moh boos-KAHR OO-nah ah-GOO-hah eh noon pah-HAHR

**He was naked!**
*¡Estaba en pelotas!*
Ehs-TAH-bah ehn peh-LOH-tahs

**You are going to bed early**
*Te acuestas con las gallinas*
Teh ah-koo-EHS-tahs kohn lahs gah-YEH-nahs

**There is no comparison between both works**
*No hay color entre los dos trabajos*
Noh AH-ee koh-LOHREHN-treh lohs dohs trah-BAH-hohs

**You must know which side one's bread is buttered on**
*Debes arrimarte al sol que más calienta*
DEH-behs ah-ree-MAHR-the ahl sohl keh mahs kah-lee-EHN-tah

**There is no solution for this**
*No hay tu tía*
Noh AH-ee too-TEE-ah

**You are well connected**
*Tienes banca*
Tee-EH-nehs BAN-kah

**I turned as red as a beetroot when she looked at me**
*Me puse rojo como un tomate cuando ella me miró*
Meh POO-seh ROH-hoh KOH-moh oon toh-MAH-the KWAHN-doh EH-yah meh mee-ROH

**I have spent the whole night without sleeping**
*He pasado toda la noche en vela*
Eh pah-SAH-doh TOH-dah lah NOH-cheh en VEH-lah

**I have to admit that I am so tightwad**
*Tengo que admitir que soy una rata*
TEHN-goh keh ahd-mee-TEER keh SOO-ee oona RAH-tah

**He slept like a log**
*Durmió a pierna suelta*
Door-mee-OH ah pee-HER-nah soo-EHL-tah

**This actor is an eye candy**
*Este actor es un bombón*
EHS-teh ahk-TOHR ehs oon bohm-BOHN

**You need to be very careful**
*Tienes que andar con pies de plomo*
Tee-EH-nehs keh ahn-DAHR- kohn pee-EHS deh PLOH-moh

**Let's take the scenic rout**
*Vamos a buscarle tres pies al gato*
VAH-mohs ah boos-KAHR-leh trehs pii-EH-lehs ahl GAH-toh

**This argument is happening without rhyme or reason**
*Esta discusión no tiene ni pies ni cabeza*
EHS-tah dees-koo-see-OHN noh tee-EH-neh nee pee-EHS nee kah-BEH-sah

**When you see a problem, you pass the bucket**
*Cuando ves un problema, te lavas las manos*
KWAHN-doh vehs oon proh-BLEH-mah the LAH-vahs lahs MAH-nohs

**It takes two to tango**
*Esto es cosa de a dos*
EHS-toh ehs KOH-sah deh  ah dohs

**You really put your feet on it this time**
*Esta vez has metido la pata hasta el fondo*
EHS-tah vehs ahs meh-TEE-doh lah PAH-tah  as tah el FOHN doh

**You have to do your homework to the T**
*Tienes que hacer tu tarea al pie de la letra*
Tee-EH-nehs keh ah-SEHR too tah-REH-ah  ahl pee-EH deh lah LEH-trah

**Good vibes**
*Buenas  vibraciones*
BWEHNash vee-bra-ZION-nehs

**They both caused a scene in public**
*Ambos montaron  una escena*
AHM-bohs mohn-TAH-rohn oona  eh SEH nah

**I am craving some cigarrettes**
*Muero por un cigarro*
moo EH roh por OON see-GAH-rroh

**Talking someone's ear off**
*Hablar hasta la saciedad*
Ah-BLAHR AHS-tah lah sah-see-EH-dahd

**Take it easy!**
*¡Tranquilo!*
tran KEE loh

**You both are inseparable**
*Son carne y uña*
son KAHR-neh OO-nyah ee

**Chug a drink (alcohol)**
*Fondo blanco*
FON doh BLAN koh

**Those shoes are the latest thing**
*Esos zapatos son el último grito*
EH-sohs sah-PAH-tohs sohn ehl OOL-tee-moh GREE-toh

**If you are going to be unhappy, don't come**
*Si vas a estar a disgusto, no vengas*
See vahs ah ehs-TAHR ah dees-GOOS-toh noh VEHN-gahs

**I am knackered**
*Estoy muy cansado*
Eh-TOH-ee MOO-ee kahn-SAH-doh

**You are cheeky**
*Eres un descarado*
EH-rehs oon dehs-kah-RAH-doh

**He has been narky the whole day**
*Ha sido un gruñón durante todo el día*
Ah SEE-doh oon groo-NYOHN doo-RAHN-teh TOH-doh ehl DEE-ah

**Can't be arsed**
*No me importa*
Noh meh eem-POHR-tah

**At the end, we are back**
*Al fin y al cabo, hemos vuelto*
Ahl feen ee ahl KAH-boh EH-mohs voo-EHL-toh

**You are swearing so much**
*Estás echando sapos y culebras*
ehs-TAHS eh-CHAHN-doh SAH-pohs ee koo-LEH-brahs

**Are you flirting with me?**
*¿Me estás cargando?*
Meh ehs-TAHS kar GAHN doh

*Brutal*
BROO-tahl

**They are looking for a fight**
*Están buscando pelea*
Ehs-TAHN boos-KAHN-doh peh LE ah

*Basta*
BAHS ta

**Hey, kid**
*Oye chico*
OH-yeh CHEE koh

**You hit the target**
*Has dado en el blanco*
Ahs DAH-doh ehn ehl BLAHN-koh

**We are so dreamy**
*Somos muy soñadores*
SOH mohs MOOee so neeah DOH rehs

**I can't stop overthinking**
*No puedo parar de pensar*
Noh PWEH-doh pah-RAHR deh PEN sahr

**I don't have money**
*No tengo un peso*
Noh TEHN-goh oon PEH soh

**You are snobbish**
*Eres un estirado*
EH-rehs oon esh tee RAH doh

**You are really old**
*Eres del año de la pera*
EH-rehs dehl AH-nyoh deh lah PEH-rah

**He is so absent-minded**
*Está en la luna*
Ehs-TAH ehn lah LOO-nah

*Me importa un carajo*
Meh eem-POHR-tah oon cah RAH ho

*Tiro la toalla*
TEE-roh lah toh-AH-yah

**This party is so cool!**
*¡Esta fiesta está bárbara!*
EHS-tah fee-EHS-tah BAHR bah rah

**Give me a beer. I need to drown my sorrows**
*Dame una cerveza. Necesito ahogar mis penas*
DAH-meh OO-nah sehr-VEH-sah neh-seh-SEE-toh ah-oh-GAHR mees PEH-nahs

**He lost the plot**
*Se puso como loco*
Seh POO-soh KOH-moh LOH-koh

**It's getting late, I better crack on**
*Se está haciendo tarde, será mejor que empiece*
Seh ehs-TAH ah-see-EHN-doh TAHR-deh seh-RAH meh-HOHR keh ehm-pee-EH-seh

**We are just taking the piss**
*Solo estamos bromeando*
SOH-loh ehs-TAH-mohs broh-meh-AHN-doh

**It is dodgy**
*No es fiable*
Noh ehs fee-AH-bleh

**I legged it from the police**
*Salí corriendo de la policía*
sah-LEE koh-rree-EHN-doh deh lah poh-lee-SEE-ah

**He was pissed**
*Estaba enojado*
Ehs-TAH-bah eno HA doh

**I have been faffing around the whole day**
*No he hecho nada en todo el día*
Noh eh EH-choh NAH-dah ehn TOH-doh ehl DEE-ah

**I feel you**
*Te entiendo*
Teh ehn-tee-EHN-doh

**Same here**
*Estoy de acuerdo*
Ehs-TOH-ee deh ah-koo-EHR-doh

**No big deal**
*Sin problema*
Seen proh-BLEH-mah

**You are cheesy**
*Eres empalagoso*
EH-rehs ehm-pah-lah-GOH-soh

**That film was a turn off**
*Esa película fue repulsiva*
EH-sah peh-LEE-koo-lah foo-EH reh-pool-SEE-vah

**I'm down**
*Me apunto*
Meh ah-POON-toh

**She dumped me**
*Ella me dejó*
EH-yah meh deh-HOH

**You are a chicken**
*Eres un gallina*
EH-rehs oon gah-YEE-nah

**He bailed me**
*Me dejó tirado*
Meh deh-HOH tee-RAH-doh

# Insults

**Shut up**
*Callate*
KAH-yah-teh

**You are such a drimwit**
*Eres un baboso*
EH-rehs oon bah-BOH-soh

**She is an opportunist**
*Es una trepadora*
Ehs oona treh pah DOH rah

**You are an idiot**
*Eres idiota*
EH-rehs ee-dee-OH-tah

**You are crazy**
*Estás loco*
Ehs-TAHS LOH-coh

**Screw you**
*Andá a cagar*
An DAH a KAH gahr

**You bastard**
*Eres un bastardo*
EH-rehs oon bahs-TAHR-doh

**You are an imbecile**
*Eres un imbécil*
EH-rehs oon eem-BEH-seel

Bitch
*Bruja*

**Stupid**
*Estúpido*
Ehs-TOO-peh-doh

**Son of a bitch**
*Hijo de puta*
EE-HOH deh POO-tah

**Dumbass**
*Tarado*
tah-RAH-doh

**You cunt**
*Forreta*
foh-RREH-tah

**Go f*ck yourself**
*Que te den*
keh teh dehn

**Up yours**
*Fodrete*
foh-DREH-teh

**F*cking**
*Puta*
POO-tah

**Slut**
*Puta*
POO-tah

**Go to hell**
*Vete al infierno*
VEH-teh ahl een-fee-EHR-poh

79

**Lazy sod**
*Inutil*
Ee-NOO-teel

**Freak**
*Nabo*
nah boh

**You are so slow**
*Lento*
LEN toh

**The lights are on but there's nobody home**
*Corto de luces*
KOHR-toh deh LOO-sehs

**You are rubbish**
*Eres una porquería*
EH-rehs OO-nah pohr-keh-REE-ah

**You are a bad person**
*Mala gente*
MAH lah hen teh

# Apologies

**Sorry**
*Perdón*
Pehr-DOHN

**I am sorry**
*Lo siento*
Loh see-EHN-toh

**I'm sorry, it won't happen again**
*Lo siento no volverá a ocurrir*
Loh see-EHN-toh noh vohl-veh-RAH ah oh-koo-RREER

**Forgive me**
*Perdóname*
Pehr-DOH-nah-meh

**Apologies for being late**
*Disculpas por llegar tarde*
Dees-KOOL-pahs pohr yeh-GAHR TAHR-deh

**I regret what I've done**
*Lamento lo que he hecho*
Lah-MEHN-toh loh keh eh EH-choh

**Sorry, but I can't today**
*Lo siento, pero hoy no puedo*
Loh see-EHN-toh PHE-roh OH-ee noh poo-EH-doh

**I hope in time we can still be friends**
*Espero que con el tiempo podamos seguir siendo amigos*
Ehs-PEH-roh keh kohn ehl tee-EHM-poh poh-DAH-mohs seh-GEER see-EHN-doh ah-MEE-gohs

**I'm deeply sorry for what's happened**
*Lamento profundamente lo que pasó*
Lah-MEHN-toh proh-foon-dah-MEHN-teh loh keh pah-SOH

**Sorry to hear the bad news**
*Lamento oír las malas noticias*
Lah-MEHN-toh oh-EER lahs MAH-lahs noh-TEE-see-ahs

**I'm so sorry about your loved one**
*Siento mucho lo de tu ser querido*
See-EHN-toh MOO-choh loh deh too sehr keh-REE-doh

**I admit it. It was my fault**
*Lo admito. Fue mi culpa*
Loh ahd-MEE-toh foo-EH mee KOOL-pah

**It wasn't your fault**
*No fue tu culpa*
Noh foo-EH too KOOL-pah

**My bad**
*Culpa mía*
KOOL-pah MEE ah

# Responses

**Don't worry**
*No te preocupes*
Noh teh preh-oh-KOO-pehs

**No problem**
*No hay problema*
Noh 'AH-ee proh-BLEH-mah

**You don't need to say sorry**
*No tienes que perdir disculpas*
Noh tee-EH-nehs keh peh-DEER dees-KOOL-pahs

**We will fix it**
*Lo arreglaremos*
Loh ah-rreh-glah-REH-mohs

**We will find a solution**
*Encontraremos una solución*
Ehn-kohn-trah-REH-mohs OO-nah soh-loo-see-OHN

**It could happen to anyone**
*Podría haberle pasado a cualquiera*
Poh-DREE-ah ah-BEHR-leh pah-SAH-doh ah koo-ahl-kee-EH-rah

**Apologies accepted**
*Disculpas aceptadas*
Dees-KOOL-pahs ah-sehp-TAH-dahs

**I'm sorry but it is nothing important**
*Lo siento, pero no es nada importante*
Loh see-EHN-toh PEH-roh noh ehs NAH-dah eem-pohr-TAHN-teh

**That sounds like an excuse**
*Suena como si fuese una excusa*
Soo-EH-nah KOH-moh see foo-EH-rah OO-nah ehks-KOO-sah

**I wish it was an excuse, but it is the truth**
*Ojalá fuera una excusa, pero es la verdad*
Oh-hah-LAH foo-EH-rah OO-nah ehks-KOO-sah PEH-roh ehs lah vehr-DAHD

# Emergencies

## Help!
*¡Ayuda!*
Ah-YOO-dah

## Please help!
*¡Ayuda por favor!*
Ah-YOO-dah pohr fah-VOHR

### Call an ambulance!
*¡Llama una ambulancia!*
YAH-mah OO-nah ahm-boo-LAHN-see-ah

### Call the police!
*¡Llama a la policía!*
YAH-mah ah lah poh-lee-SEE-ah

### There has been an accident, call an ambulance quickly!
*¡ Hubo un accidente, llama a una ambulancia rápidamente!*
OO boh oon ahk-see-DEHN-teh YAH-mah ah OO-nah ahm-boo-LAHN-see-ah rah-peh-dah-MEHN-teh

### I need to go to the hospital
*Necesito ir al hospital*
Neh-seh-SEE-toh eer ahl OHS-pee-tahl

### I need a doctor, quick!
*Necesito un doctor, ¡ Rápido!*
Neh-seh-SEE-toh oon dohk-TOHR RAH-pee-doh

### My handbag has been stolen!
*¡Me han robado el bolso!*
Meh ahn roh-BAH-doh ehl BOHL-soh

### I want to report a crime
*Quiero denunciar un delito*
Kee-EH-roh deh-noon-see-AHR oon deh-LEE-toh

### I want to report a robbery
*Quiero denunciar un robo*
Kee-EH-roh deh-noon-see-AHR oon ROH-boh

### I have been robbed!
*¡Me han robado!*
Meh ahn roh-BAH-doh

### My passport has been stolen!
*¡Me han robado el pasaporte!*
Meh ahn roh-BAH-doh ehl pah sah-POHR-teh

### I have been scammed
*Me han estafado*
Meh ahn ehs-tah-FAH-doh

### I need help right away
*Necesito ayuda de inmediato*
Neh-seh-SEE-toh ah-YOO-dah deh een-meh-dee-AH-toh

### You have my support
*Tienes mi apoyo*
Tee-EH-nehs mee ah-POH-yoh

### He's having a heart attack!
*¡Está teniendo un ataque al corazón!*
Ehs-TAH teh-nee-EHN-doh oon ah-TAH-keh ahl coh-rah-SOHN

**He is not breathing!**
*¡No está respirando!*
Noh ehs-TAH rehs-pee-RAHN-doh

**Stop! Thief!**
¡ Alto! ¡Ladrón!
AL toh lah-DROHN

**Show me what you have in your hand**
*Enséñame lo que tienes en tu mano*
Ehn-SEH-nyah-meh loh keh tee-EH-nehs ehn too MAH-noh

*¡Cuidado!*
koo-ee-DAH-doh

**I'm here, please help me!**
*Estoy aquí ¡ Ayuda por favor!*
Ehs-TOH-ee ah-KEE ah-YOO-dah pohr fah-VOHR

**Be careful!**
*¡Ten cuidado!*
Tehn koo-ee-DAH-doh

**Fire! Fire!**
*¡Fuego! ¡Fuego!*
foo-EH-goh foo-EH-goh

**Call the fire brigade!**
*¡Llama a los bomberos!*
YAH-mah ah lohs bohm-BEH-rohs

**The buildings on fire!**
*¡El edificio está en llamas!*
Ehl eh-dee-FEE-see-oh ehs-TAH ehn YAH-mahs

**It's an emergency!**
*¡Es una emergencia!*
Ehs OO-nah eh-mehr-HEHN-see-ah

**Does anyone know CPR?**
*¿Alguien sabe RCP?*
ahl-GEE-ehn SAH-beh ehrreh seh peh

**He is choking!**
*¡Se está ahogando!*
Seh ehs-TAH ah-oh-GAHN-doh

**Is everyone okay?**
*¿Está todo el mundo bien?*
ehs-TAH TOH-doh ehl MOON-doh bee-EHN

**She fainted**
*Se ha desmayado*
Seh ah dehs-mah-YAH-doh

**Do you have a pad?**
*¿Tienes una compresa?*
Tee-EH-nehs OO-nah kohm-PREH-sah

**Do you have tampons?**
*¿Tienes tampones?*
Tee-EH-nehs tahm-POH-nehs

**I want condoms**
*Quiero preservativos*
Kee-EH-roh preh-sehr-vah-TEE-vohs

**Her waters just broke**
*Ha roto aguas*
Ah ROH-toh AH-gwahs

**How did the accident happen?**
*¿Cómo ocurrió el accidente?*
KOH-moh oh-koo-rree-OH ehl ahk-see-DEHN-teh

**The police are urgently looking for a suspect**
*La policía está buscando un sospechoso urgentemente*
Lah poh-lee-SEE-ah ehs-TAH boos-KAHN-doh oon sohs-peh-CHOH-soh oor-hehn-teh-MEHN-teh

**Where is the lifeguard?**
*¿Dónde está el socorrista?*
DOHN-deh ehs-TAH ehl soh-koh-RREES-tah

**Someone is drowning in the pool!**
*¡Alguien se está ahogando en la piscina!*
AHL-gee-ehn seh ehs-TAH ah-oh-GAHN-doh ehn lah pees-SEE-nah

**Does anyone have a life jacket?**
*¿Alguien tiene un chaleco salvavidas?*
AHL-gee-ehn tee-EH-neh oon chah-LEH-koh sahl-vah-VEE-dahs

# Medical

**I don't feel well**
*No me encuentro bien*
Noh meh ehn-koo-EHN-troh bee-EHN

**I have to go to the doctor**
*Tengo que ir al médico*
TEHN-goh keh eer ahl MEH-dee-koh

Ouch, that hurts
*Ay, me duele*
*AH-ee meh doo-EH-leh*

**I have a fever**
*Tengo fiebre*
TEHN-goh fee-EH-breh

**I have a pain here**
*Me duele aquí*
Meh doo-EH-leh ah-KEE

**I have a headache**
*Me duele la cabeza*
Meh doo-EH-leh lah kah-BEH-sah

**She has cancer**
*Ella tiene cáncer*
EH-yah tee-EH-neh KAHN-sehr

**Where is the closest hospital?**
*¿Dónde está el hospital más cercano?*
DOHN-deh ehs-TAH ehl ohs-pee-TAHL mahs sehr-KAH-noh

**Is there a 24-hour doctor close by?**
*¿Hay algún médico 24 horas cerca?*
AH-ee ahl-GOON MEH-dee-koh 24 OH-rahs SEHR-kah

**Does the doctor do callouts?**
*¿El médico hace visitas?*
Ehl MEH-dee-koh AH-seh vee SEE tahs

**I have health insurance**
*Tengo seguro médico*
TEHN-goh seh-GOO-roh MEH-dee-koh

84

**I have travel insurance**
*Tengo seguro de viaje*
TEHN-goh seh-GOO-roh deh vee-AH-heh

**I need medication**
*Necesito medicación*
Neh-seh-SEE-toh meh-dee-kah-see-OHN

**I have a prescription**
*Tengo una receta*
TEHN-goh OO-nah reh-SEE-tah

**My stomach hurts**
*Me duele el estómago*
Meh doo-EH-leh ehl ehs-TOH-mah-goh

**I think I am dehydrated**
*Creo que estoy deshidratado*
KREH-oh keh ehs-TOO-eh dehs-ee-drah-TAH-doh

**Do you drink enough water?**
*¿Bebes suficiente agua?*
BEH-behs soo-fee-see-EHN-teh AH-gwah

**Heatstroke**
*Ataque al corazón*
Ah-TAH-keh ahl koh-rah-SOHN

**Sprained ankle**
*Esguince de tobillo*
Ehs-GEEN-seh deh toh BEE-yoh

**Is the bone broken?**
*¿Está roto el hueso?*
Ehs-TAH ROH-toh ehl hoo-EH-soh

**I'm allergic to…**
*Soy alérgico a…*
SOH-ee ah-LEHR-hee-koh ah

**I think I ate something bad**
*Creo que he comido algo en mal estado*
KREH-oh keh eh koh-MEE-doh AHL-goh ehn mahl ehs-TAH-doh

**Is there a pharmacy nearby?**
*¿Hay alguna farmacia cerca?*
AH-ee ahl-GOO-nah fahr-MAH-see-ah SEHR-kah

**How long will I take to recover?**
*¿Cuánto tiempo tardaré en recuperarme?*
KWAHN-toh tee-EHM-poh tahr-dah-REH ehn reh-koo-peh-RAHR-meh

**Can I get crutches, please?**
*¿Me das muletas por favor?*
Meh dahs moo-LEH-tahs pohr fah-VOHR

**Can I get a wheelchair, please?**
*¿Me das una silla de ruedas por favor?*
Meh dahs OO-nah SEE-yah deh roo-EH-dahs pohr fah-VOHR

**I have diarrhea**
*Tengo diarrea*
TEHN-goh dee ah-RREH-ah

**How much does an operation cost?**
*¿Cuánto cuesta una operación?*
KWAHN-toh koo-EHS-tah OO-nah oh-peh-rah-see-OHN

**Is the public service better than the private?**
*¿Es el servicio público mejor que el privado?*
Ehs ehl sehr-VEE-see-oh POO-blee-koh meh-HOHR keh ehl pree-VAH-doh

**How much does the dentist cost here?**
*¿Cuánto cuesta el dentista aquí?*
KWAHN-toh koo-EHS-tah ehl dehn-TEES-tah ah-KEE

**I have a private insurance**
*Tengo seguro privado*
TEHN-goh seh-GOO-roh pree-VAH-doh

**I need to get my wisdom tooth removed**
*Tengo que sacarme la muela de juicio*
TEHN-goh keh sah-KAHR-meh lah moo-EH-lah deh hoo-EE-see-oh

**She will wear braces soon**
*Ella llevará brackets pronto*
EH-yah yeh-vah-RAH BRAH-kehts PROHN-toh

**I have lost my hearing**
*He perdido la audición*
Eh pehr-DEE-doh lah ah-OO-dee-see-OHN

**I need an hearing aid**
*Necesito un audífono*
Neh-seh-SEE-toh oon ah-oh-DEE-foh-noh

**Can I get an appointment for the dermatologist?**
*¿Puedo marcar una cita con el dermatólogo?*
Poo-EH-doh MARK ahr OO-nah SEE-tah kohn ehl dehr-mah-TOH-loh-goh

**I have so many spots**
*Tengo muchos granos*
TEHN-goh MOO-chohs GRAH-nohs

**I have marks in my face**
*Tengo marcas en la cara*
TEHN-goh MAHR-kahs ehn lah KAH-rah

**My mum is losing her sight**
*Mi madre está perdiendo la vista*
Mee MAH-dreh ehs-TAH pehr-dee-EHN-doh lah VEES-tah

**He / She needs glasses**
Necesita gafas
Neh-seh-SEE-tah GAH-fahs

**Let's get an appointment with the optician**
*Vamos marcar cita con la óptica*
VAH-mohs ah MARK ahr SEE-tah kohn lah OHP-tee-kah

**I prefer wearing contact lenses**
*Prefiero usar lentillas*
Preh-fee-EH-roh oo-SAHR lehn-TEE-yahs

**I have been vomiting**
*He estado vomitando*
Eh ehs-TAH-doh voh-mee-TAHN-doh

**Get well soon**
*Que te mejores pronto*
Keh teh meh-HOH-rehs PROHN-toh

**I have burned myself**
*Me he quemado*
Meh eh keh-MAH-doh

**Are there any alternative treatments?**
*¿Hay algún tratamiento alternativo?*
AH-ee ahl-GOON trah-tah-mee-EHN-toh ahl-tehr-nah-TEE-voh

**Do you have any painkillers?**
*¿Tiene algún analgésico?*
Tee-EH-neh ahl-GOON ah-nahl-HEH-see-koh

**Do you have plasters?**
*¿Tienes curitas?*
Tee-EH-nehs koo-REE-tahs

**I had an abortion**
*Tuve un aborto*
TOO-veh oon ah-BOHR-toh

**Do you have a medical kit?**
*¿Tienes un botiquín?*
Tee-EH-nehs oon boh tee KEEN

**I think I am pregnant**
*Creo que estoy embarazada*
KREH-oh keh ehs-TOH-ee ehm-bah-rah-SAH-dah

**Can I get the contraceptive pills, please?**
*¿Me das píldoras anticonceptivas por favor?*
Meh dahs PEEL-doh-rahs ahn-tee-cohn-sehp-TEE-vahs por fah VOR

**I want to go to the gynecologist**
*Quiero ir al ginecólogo*
Kee-EH-roh eer ahl hee-neh-KOH-loh-goh

**Do you take any medication?**
*¿Tienes alguna medicación?*
Tee-EH-nehs ahl-GOO-nah meh-dee-kah-see-OHN

# Animals

**Cats are so independent**
*Los gatos son muy independientes*
Lohs GAH-toh sohn MOO-ee een dch pehn-dee-EHN-tehs

**The dog is a man's best friend**
*El perro es el mejor amigo del hombre*
Ehl PEH-rroh ehs ehl meh-HOHR ah-MEE-goh dehl OHM-breh

**Birds fly**
*Los pájaros vuelan*
Lohs PAH-hah-rohs voo-EH-lahn

**Parrots repeat what you say**
*Los loros repiten lo que dices*
Lohs LOH-rohs reh-PEE-tehn loh keh DEE-sehs

**Frogs jump high**
*Las ranas saltan alto*
Lahs RAH-nah SAHL-tahn AHL-toh

**Horses are strong**
*Los caballos son fuertes*
Lohs kah-BAH-yohs sohn foo-EHR-tehs

**The goat climbs mountains**
*La cabra escala montañas*
Lah KAH-brah ehs-KAH-lah mohn-TAH-nyahs

**That fly is disgusting**
*Esa mosca es asquerosa*
EH-sah MOHS-kah ehs ahs-keh-ROH-sah

**The fish live in water**
*El pez vive en el agua*
ehl pehs VEE-veh ehn ehl AH-gwah

**The shark is a predator**
*El tiburón es un depredador*
Ehl tee-boo-ROHN ehs oon deh-preh-dah-DOHR

**The whale is a mammal**
*La ballena es un mamífero*
Lah bah-YEH-nah ehs oon mah-MEE-feh-roh

**Octopus have 8 tentacles**
*Los pulpos tienen 8 tentáculos*
Lohs POOL-pohs tee-EH-nehn 8 tehn-TAH-koo-lohs

**Rabbits are small**
*Los conejos son pequeños*
Lohs koh-NEH-hohs sohn peh-KEH-nyos

**Sheep are very soft**
*Las ovejas son muy suaves*
Lahs oh-VEH-hahs sohn MOO-ee soo-AH-vehs

**The chicken has good meat**
*El pollo tiene buena carne*
Ehl POH-yoh tee-EH-neh boo-EH-nah KAHR-neh

**Pigs are dirty**
*Los cerdos son sucios*
Lohs CEHR-dohs sohn SOO-see-ohs

**Fox is intelligent**
*El zorro es inteligente*
Ehl SOH-rroh ehs een-teh-lee-HEHN-teh

**Lion is the king of the jungle**
*El león es el rey de la jungla*
Ehl leh-OHN ehs ehl REH-ee deh lah HOON-glah

**The trump of the elephant is big**
*La trompa del elefante es grande*
Lah TROHM-pah dehl Eh-leh-FAHN-teh ehs GRAHN-deh

**Giraffe is very tall**
*La Jirafa es muy alta*
Lah hee-RAH-fah ehs MOO-ee AHL-tah

**The cheetah is very silent**
*El guepardo es muy silencioso*
Ehl geh-PAHR-doh ehs MOO-ee see-lehn-see-OH-soh

**Hippos are aggressive**
*Los hipopótamos son agresivos*
Lohs ee-poh-POH-tah-mohs sohn ah-greh-SEE-vohs

**That monkey looks like a human**
*Ese mono parece un humano*
EH-seh MOH-noh pah-REH-seh oon ooh-MAH-noh

**That bear looks hungry**
*Ese oso parece hambriento*
EH-seh OH-soh pah-REH-seh ahm-bree-EHN-toh

**Rhinos have horns**
*Los rinocerontes tienen cuernos*
Lohs ree-noh-seh-ROHN-tehs tee-EH-nehn koo-EHR-nohs

**They are farm animals**
*Son animales de granja*
Sohn ah-nee-MAH-lehs deh GRAHN-hah

**They are wild animals**
*Son animales salvajes*
Sohn ah-nee-MAH-lehs sahl-VAH-hehs

**The fur of the fox is brown**
*El pelaje del zorro es marrón*
Ehl peh-LAH-heh dehl SOH-rroh ehs mah-RROHN

**The birds are covered in feathers**
*Los pájaros están cubiertos de plumas*
Lohs PAH-hah-rohs ehs-TAHN koo-bee-EHR-tohs deh PLOO-mahs

**Cats have 4 paws**
*Los gatos tienen 4 patas*
Lohs GAH-tohs tee-EH-nehn 4 PAH-tahs

**They need wings to fly**
*Necesitan alas para volar*
Neh-seh-SEE-tahn AH-lahs PAH-rah voh-LAHR

**The tigers use their fangs to eat meat**
*Los tigres usan sus colmillos para comer carne*
Lohs TEE-grehs OO-sahn soos kohl-MEE-yohs PAH-rah koh-MEHR KAHR-neh

**Have you bought cat's food?**
*¿Has comprado comida para gatos?*
Ahs kohm-PRAH-doh koh-MEE-dah PAH-rah GAH-tohs

**We adopted him in an animal shelter**
*Lo adoptamos en un refugio animal*
Loh ah-dohp-TAH-mohs ehn oon reh-FOO-hee-oh ah-nee-MAHL

**Aquarius are always busy**
*Los acuarios siempre están llenos*
Lohs ah-koo-AH-ree-ohs see-EHM-preh ehs-TAHN YEH-nohs

**The cows live on the field**
*Las vacas viven en el campo*
Lahs VAH-kahs VEE-vehn ehn ehl KAHM-poh

**He needs a bigger cage**
*Necesita una jaula más grande*
Neh-seh-SEE-tah OO-nah HAH-oo-lah mahs GRAHN-deh

**My cat is going to have kittens**
*Mi gata va a tener gatitos*
Mee GAH-tah vah ah teh-NEHR gah-TEE-tohs

**His dog is going to have puppies**
*Su perra va a tener cachorros*
Soo PEH-rrah vah ah teh-NEHR kah-CHOH-rrohs

You need to put the turtle in the pond
*Tienes que poner la tortuga en el estanque*
Tee-EH-nehs keh poh-NEHR lah tohr-TOO-gah ehn ehl ehs-TAHN-keh

You need to take the bull by the horns
*Tienes que tomar el toro por los cuernos*
Tee-EH-nehs keh toh MAHR ehl TOH-roh pohr lohs koo-EHR-nohs

Recicling is very important
*Reciclar es muy importante*
Reh-see-KLAHR ehs MOO-ee eem-pohr-THAN-teh

You have to clean your pet
*Tienes que limpiar a tu mascota*
Tee-EH-nehs keh leem-pee-AHR ah too mahs-KOH-tah

The pot calling the kettle black
*El burro hablando de sus orejas*
Ehl BOO-rroh ah-BAHN-doh deh soos oh REH-hahs

Beaks are different
*Los picos son diferentes*
Lohs PEE-koh sohn dee-feh-REHN-tehs

I need to take my pet to the vet
*Necesito llevar a mi mascota al veterinario*
Neh-seh-SEE-toh yeh-VAHR ah mee mahs-KOH-tah ahl veh-teh-ree-NAH-ree-oh

We sell collars for dogs
*Vendemos collares para perros*
Vehn-DEH-mohs koh-YAH-rehs PAH-rah PEH-rrohs

We should go to the zoo
*Deberíamos ir al zoo*
Deh-beh-REE-ah-mohs eer ahl soo

# Places and Activities

We should go to the beach
*Deberíamos ir a la playa*
Deh-beh-REE-ah-mohs eer ah la PLAH-yah

I want to sunbathe
*Quiero tomar sol*
Kee-EH-roh toh-MAHR sohl

We did parachuting
*Hicimos paracaidismo*
Eeh-SEEH-mohs pah-rah-kah-ee-DEES-moh

Have you visited this mountain?
*¿Has visitado esta montaña?*
Ahs vee-see-TAH-doh EHS-tah mohn-TAH-nyah

Ice skating is not for summer
*El patinaje sobre hielo no es para verano*
Ehl pah-tee-NAH-heh SOH-breh ee-EH-loh noh ehs PAH-rah veh-RAH-noh

Bowling is not an individual activity
*Los bolos no son una actividad individual*
Lohs BOH-lohs noh sohn OO-nah ahk-tee-vee-DAHD een-dee-vee-doo-AHL

Paddle tennis is very common in Spain
*El pádel es muy común en España*
Ehl PAH-dehl ehs MOO-ee koh-MOON ehn ehs-PAH-nyah

We need to rent a boat for that lake
*Necesitamos alquilar una barca para ese lago*
Neh-seh-see-TAH-mohs ahl-kee-LAHR OO-nah BAHR-kah porh EHS-seh LAH-goh

I got lost in that forest
*Me perdí en ese bosque*
Meh pehr-DEE ehn EH-seh BOHS-keh

Let's go camping
*Vamos de acampada*
VAH-mohs deh ah-kahm-PAH-dah

I go to church every Sunday
*Voy a la iglesia todos los domingos*
VOH-ee ah lah ee-GLEH-see-ah TOH-dohs lohs doh-MEEN-gohs

Let's go diving
*Vamos a bucear*
VAH-mohs ah boo-seh-AHR

We have to explore the city
*Tenemos que explorar la ciudad*
Teh-NEH-mohs keh ehks-ploh-RAHR lah see-oo-DAHD

They are going to the concert
*Ellos van al concierto*
EH-yohs vahn ahl kohn-see-EHR-toh

I want to swim in the sea
*Quiero nadar en el mar*
Kee-EH-roh nah-DAHR ehn ehl bahr

She only wants to play videogames
*Ella solo quiere jugar a los videojuegos*
EH-yah SOH-loh kee-EH-reh hoo-GAHR ah lohs vee-deh-oh-hoo-EH-gohs

I need to relax in a spa
*Necesito relajarme en un spa*
Neh-seh-SEE-toh reh-lah-HAHR-meh ehn oon Ehs-PAH

Take pictures of that building
*Toma fotos de ese edificio*
TOH mah FOH-tohs deh EH-seh eh-dee-FEE-see-oh

That desert is so big
*Ese desierto es muy grande*
EH-seh deh-see-EHR-toh ehs MOO-ee GRAHN-deh

let's swim in this river
*Vamos a nadar en este río*
VAH-mohs ah nah-DAHE ehn EHS-teh REE-oh

The film will end soon
*La película acabará pronto*
Lah peh-LEE-koo-lah ah-kah-bah-RAH PROHN-toh

The ocean is so transparent
*El océano es muy transparente*
Ehl oh-SEH-ah-noh ehs MOO-ee trahns-pah-REHN-teh

**I would like to visit an island**
*Me gustaría visitar una isla*
Meh goos tah REE ah vee-see-TAHR
OO-nah EES-lah

**Have you ever seen a volcano?**
*¿Has visto algún volcán?*
Ahs VEES-toh ahl-GOON vohl-KAHN

**That animal doesn't belong to the jungle**
*Ese animal no pertenece a la jungla*
EH-seh ah-nee-MAHL noh pehr-teh-
NEH-seh ah lah HOON-glah

**Visiting places opens your mind**
*Visitar lugares abre tu mente*
Vee-see-TAHR loo-GAH-rehs AH-breh
too MEHN-teh

**My daughter built a sandcastle**
Mi hija construyó un castillo de arena
Mee EE-hah cohns-troo-YOH oon kahs-
TEE-yoh deh ah-REH-nah

**He likes to splash in the swimming pool**
*Le gusta salpicar en la piscina*
Leh GOOS-tah sahl-pee-KAHR ehn lah
pees-SEE-nah

**You need to make sure that you know where the life jackets are**
*Tienes que asegurarte de saber dónde están los chalecos sal-vavidas*
Tee-EH-nehs keh ah-seh-goo-RAHR-teh
deh sah BEHR DOHN-deh ehs-TAHN
lohs chah-LEH-kohs sahl-vah-VEE-dahs

**We can rent a jet ski**
*Podemos alquilar una moto agua*
Poh-DEH-mohs ahl-kee-LAHR OO
MOH-toh deh AH-goo-ah

**Time to hit the beach!**
*¡Es hora de ir a la playa!*
Ehs OH-rah deh eer ah lah PLAH-yah

**The cave is so old**
*La cueva es muy antigua*
Lah koo-EH-vah ehs MOO-ee ahn-TEE-
goo-ah

**Waterfalls are beautiful**
*Las cascadas son hermosas*
Lahs Kahs-KAH-dah sohn ehr-MOH-sahs

**We can camp here**
*Podemos acampar aquí*
Poh-DEH-mohs ah-kahm-PAHR ah-KEE

**I want to go climbing**
*Quiero escalar*
Kee-EH-roh ehs-kah-LAHR

**I don't like hunting**
*No me gusta cazar*
Noh meh GOOS-tah kah-SAHR

# Feelings

I am tired
*Estoy cansado*
Ehs-TOH-ee kahn-SAH-doh

I feel bad
*Me siento mal*
Meh see-EHN-toh mahl

I am really happy
*Estoy muy contenta (feminine)*
Ehs-TOH-ee MOO-ee kohn-TEHN-tah

I am really happy
*Estoy muy contento (masculine)*
Ehs-TOH-ee MOO-ee kohn-TEHN-toh

I am shy
*Soy tímido (masculine)*
SOH-ee TEE-mee-doh

I am shy
*Soy tímida (feminine)*
SOH-ee TEE-mee-dah

He is very patient
*Es muy paciente*
ehs MOO-ee pah-see-EHN-teh

We are calm
*Estamos calmados*
Ehs-TAH-mohs kahl-MAH-dohs

I am glad
*Me alegro*
Meh ah-LEH-groh

You look serious
*Estás serio*
Ehs-TAHS SEH-ree-oh

I am starving
*Estoy hambriento*
Ehs-TOH-ee ahm-bree-EHN-toh

I am in love
*Estoy enamorada (feminine)*
Ehs-TOH-ee eh-nah-moh-RAH-dah

I am in love
*Estoy enamorado (masculine)*
Ehs-TOH-ee eh-nah-moh-RAH-doh

How do you feel?
*¿Cómo te sientes?*
KOH-moh teh see-EHN-tehs

What do you feel?
*¿Qué sientes?*
Keh see-EHN-tehs

Are you falling in love?
*¿Te estás enamorando?*
Teh ehs-TAHS eh-nah-moh-RAHN-doh

Why are you crying?
*¿Por qué estás llorando?*
Pohr keh ehs-TAHS yoh-RAHN-doh

I don't feel really good
*No me encuentro bien*
Noh meh ehn-koo-EHN-troh bee-EHN

93

**He is anxious**
*Está ansioso*
Ehs-TAH ahn-see-OH-soh

**This motivates me**
*Esto me motiva*
EHS-toh meh moh-TEE-vah

**I feel betrayed**
*Me siento traicionada (feminine)*
Meh see-EHN-toh trah-ee-see-oh-NAH-dah

**I feel betrayed**
*Me siento traicionado (masculine)*
Meh see-EHN-toh trah-ee-see-oh-NAH-doh

**I feel bad for you**
*Me siento mal por ti*
Meh see-EHN-toh mahl pohr tee

**I am proud of you**
*Estoy orgullosa de ti (feminine)*
Ehs-TOH-ee ohr-goo-YOH-sah deh tee

**I am proud of you**
*Estoy orgulloso de ti (masculine)*
Ehs-TOH-ee ohr-goo-YOH-soh deh tee

**Is it hard for you?**
*¿Es duro para ti?*
Ehs DOO-roh PAH-rah tee

**I cannot trust you**
*No puedo confiar en ti*
Noh poo-EH-doh kohn-fee-AHR ehn tee

**You are reliable**
*Eres fiable*
EH-rehs fee-AH-bleh

**Do you love me?**
*¿Me quieres?*
Meh kee-EH-rehs

**That makes me sad**
*Eso me pone triste*
EH-soh meh POH-neh TREES-teh

**He is very quiet**
*Es muy callado*
Ehs MOO-ee kah-YAH-doh

**You hurt me!**
*¡Me hiciste daño!*
Meh ee-SEEHS-teh DAH-nyoh

**It is such a pain!**
*¡Es tan doloroso!*
Ehs TAHN doh-loh-ROH-soh

**You hurt my feelings**
*Has herido mis sentimientos*
Ahs eh-REE-doh mees sehn-tee-mee-EHN-tohs

**You broke my heart**
*Me rompiste el corazón*
Meh rohm-PEES-teh ehl koh-rah-SOHN

# House

Do you pay a loan for the house?
*¿Pagas una cuota por tu casa?*
PAH-gahs oonah KWO tah pohr too KAH-sah

Are you planning on selling this house?
*¿Estás pensando vender esta casa?*
Ehs-TAHS pehn-SAHN-doh vehn-DEHR EHS-tah KAH-sah

I want to buy a flat
*Quiero comprare un piso*
Kee-EH-roh kohm-PRAHR- oon PEE-soh

I thought it was a bungalow
*Pensaba que era un bungaló*
Pehn-SAH-bah keh EH-rah oon boon-gah-LOH

That wardrobe is new
*Ese armario es nuevo*
EH-she ahr-MAH-ree-oh ehs noo-EH-voh

Redecorating the house is a good idea
*Redecorar la casa es una buena idea*
Reh-deh-koh-RAHR lah KAH-sah chs OO-nah BOOE nah ee-DEH-ah

We should mow the grass
*Deberíamos cortar el césped*
Deh-beh-REE-ah-mohs kohr-TAHR ehl SEHS-pehd

How is the house market at the moment?
*¿Cómo está el mercado de casas por el momento?*
KOH-moh ehs-TAH ehl mehr-KAH-doh deh KAH-sahs pohr ehl moh-MEHN-toh

Do you share accommodation?
*¿Compartes casa?*
Kohm-PAHR-tehs KAH-sah

How are your flatmates?
*¿Cómo son tus compañeros de piso?*
KOH-moh sohn toos kohm-pah-NYEH-rohs deh PEE-soh

Are you renting?
*¿Estás alquilando?*
Ehs-TAHS deh ahl-kee LAH ndo

How much is your rent per month?
*¿Cuánto pagas de alquiler al mes?*
KWAHN-toh PAH-gahs deh ahl-kee-LEHR ahl mehs

This is the first floor
*Esta es la primera planta*
EHS-tah ehs lah pree-MEH-rah PLAHN-tah

That is the ground floor
*Esa es la planta baja*
EH-sah ehs lah PLAHN-tah BAH-hah

## We don't have underground floor
*No tenemos sótano*
Noh teh-NEH-mohs SOH-tah-noh

## Have you set the alarm?
*¿Has activado la alarma?*
Ahs ahk-tee-VAH-doh lah ah-LAHR-mah

## No one can come in
*Nadie puede entrar*
NAH-dee-eh poo-EH-deh ehn-TRAHR

## You can wait in the living room
*Puedes esperar en el salón*
PWEH-dehs ehs-peh-RAHR ehn ehl sah-LOHN

## If you want water, go to the kitchen
*Si quieres agua, ve a la cocina*
See kee-EH-rehs AH-goo-ah veh ah lah koh-SEE-nah

## I need to go to the restroom urgently
*Necesito ir al baño urgentemente*
Neh-seh-SEE-toh eer ahl BAH-nyoh oor-hehn-teh-MEHN-teh

## I'm going to park my car in your garage
*Voy a aparcar mi coche en tu garage*
VOH-ee ah ah-pahr-KAHR mee KOH-cheh ehn too gah-RAH-heh

## Which one is your bedroom?
*¿Cuál es tu cuarto?*
Koo-AHL ehs too coo-AHR-toh

## Can you give me a towel?
*¿Puedes darme una toalla?*
PWEH dehs DAHR-meh OO-nah toh-AH-yah

## The toilet sit is dirty
*El váter está sucio*
Ehl VAH-tehr ehs-TAH SOO-see-oh

## Is there anyone in the shower?
*¿Hay alguien en la ducha?*
AH-ee AHL-gee-ehn ehn lah DOO-chah

## Where is the mirror?
*¿Dónde está el espejo?*
*DOHN-deh ehs-TAH ehl e*hs-PEH-hoh

## Turn on the heater, please
*Enciende la calefacción por favor*
Ehn-see-EHN-deh lah kah leh fahk SEEON pohr fah-VOHR

## There is no hot water
*No hay agua caliente*
Noh AH-ee AH-gwah kah-lee-EHN-teh

## I need to buy a new sponge
*Necesito comprar una esponja nueva*
Neh-seh-SEE-toh kohm-PRAHR- OO-nah ehs-POHN-hah noo-EH-vah

## The water is cold!
*¡El agua está fría!*
Ehl AH-gwah ehs-TAH FREE-ah

## Save me a sit on the couch
*Guárdame un sitio en el sofá*
GWAHR-dah-meh oon SEE-tee-oh ehn ehl soh-FAH

**I want to change the color of the walls**
*Quiero cambiar el color de las paredes*
Kee-EH-roh kahm-bee-AHR ehl koh-LOHR deh lahs pah-REH-dehs

**We need to iron the shirt**
*Necesitamos planchar la camisa*
Neh-seh-see-TAH-mohs plahn-CHAHR lah kah-MEH-sah

**Do you have an iron and an ironing board?**
*¿Tienes plancha y tabla de planchar?*
Tee-EH-nehs PLAHN-chah ee TAH-blah deh plahn-CHAHR

**Give me a cushion**
*Dame un cojín*
DAH-meh oon coh-HEEN

**That is my chair**
*Esa es mi silla*
EH-sah ehs mee SEE-yah

**turn on the lamp**
*Enciende la lámpara*
Ehn-see-EHN-deh lah LAHM-pah-rah

**Put your book on the bedside table**
*Pon tu libro en la mesa de noche*
Pohn too LEE-broh ehn lah MEH-sah deh NOH-cheh

**I am in bed**
*Estoy en la cama*
Ehs-TOH-ee ehn lah KAH-mah

**Open the window**
*Abre la ventana*
AH-breh lah vehn-TAH-nah

**Leave the door open**
*Deja la puerta abierta*
DEH-hah lah poo-EHR-tah ah-bee-EHR-tah

**Close the door**
*Cierra la puerta*
see-EH-rrah lah poo-EHR-tah

**There is someone at the door**
*Hay alguien en la puerta*
AH-ee AHL-gee-ehn ehn lah poo-EHR-tah

**Could you bring a spoon, please?**
*¿Puedes traer una cuchara por favor?*
PWEH-dehs trah-EHR OO-nah coo-CHAH-rah pohr fah-VOHR

**I don't want that plate**
*No quiero ese plato*
Noh kee-EH-roh EH-seh PLAH-toh

**Pass me a fork, please**
*Pásame un tenedor por favor*
PAH-sah-meh oon teh-NEH-dohr pohr fah-VOHR

**Give me that knife**
*Dame ese cuchillo*
DAH-mch EH-seh koo-CHEH-yoh

**I want a clean glass**
*Quiero un vaso limpio*
Kee-EH-roh oon VAH-soh LEEM-pee-oh

**You must cook the food in a pan**

*Debes cocinar la comida en una sartén*

DEH-behs koh-see-NAHR lah koh-MEE-dah ehn OO-nah sahr-TEHN

**Put the tin next to the bin**

*Pon la lata al lado de la basura*

Pohn lah LAH-tah ahl LAH-doh deh lah bah-SOO-rah

**You have to turn on the oven**

*Debes encender el horno*

DEH-behs ehn-sehn-DEHR ehl OHR-noh

**The beer is in the fridge**

*La cerveza está en la heladera*

Lah sehr-VEH-sah ehs-TAH ehn lah eh lah DEH rah

**The soup is in the microwave**

*La sopa está en el microondas*

Lah SOH-pah ehs-TAH ehn ehl mee-croh-OHN-dahs

**The tap doesn't work**

*El grifo no funciona*

Ehl GREE-foh noh foon-see-OH-nah

**Put the bread in the toaster**

*Pon el pan en la tostadora*

Pohn ehl pahn ehn lah tohs-tah-DOH-rah

**The clothes are in the washing machine**

*La ropa está en la lavadora*

lah ROH pah ehs-TAH en lah Lah-vah-DOH-rah

**Did you turn off the coffee machine?**

*¿Apagaste la cafetera?*

Ah-pah-GAHS-teh lah kah-feh-TEH-rah

# Transport

**Did you catch the plane?**

*¿Tomaste el avión?*

toh MAHS teh ehl ah-vee-OHN

**Is this a new car?**

*¿Es un coche nuevo?*

Ehs oon KOH-cheh noo-EH-voh

**I prefer a motorbike**

*Prefiero una moto*

Preh-fee-EH-roh OO-nah MOH-toh

**How much does the parking cost?**

*¿Cuánto cuesta el aparcamiento?*

KWAHN-toh koo-EHS-tah ehl ah-pahr-kah-mee-EHN-toh

**We should rent a bike**

*Deberíamos alquilar una bicicleta*

Deh-beh-REE-ah-mohs ahl-kee-LAHR OO-nah bee-see-KLEH-tah

### I like your scooter
*Me gusta tu patineta*
Meh GOOS-tah too pah-tee-NEH-tah

### That truck is too big
*Ese camión es demasiado grande*
EH-seh kah-mee-OHN ehs deh-mah-see-AH-doh GRAHN-deh

### Let's buy a caravan
*Vamos a comprar una caravana*
VAH-mohs ah Kohm-PRAHR OO-nah kah-rah-VAH-nah

### The tractor is in the field
*El tractor está en el campo*
Ehl trahk-TOHR ehs-TAH ehn ehl KAHM-poh

### The train leaves at eight
*El tren sale a las 8*
Ehl trehn SAH-leh ah lahs 8

### The trip is being delayed
*El viaje está atrasado*
Ehl vee-AH-heh ehs-TAH ah-trah-SAH-doh

### That is the boat I like
*Ese es el barco que me gusta*
EH-seh ehs ehl BAHR-coh keh me GOOS-tah

### I want to go on a cruise
*Quiero ir a un crucero*
Kee-EH-roh eer ah oon kroo-SEH-roh

### That is a bus stop
*Esta es una parada de bus*
EHS-tah ehs OO-nah pah-RAH-dah deh boos

### Can the helicopter land here?
*¿Puede el helicóptero aterrizar aquí?*
PWEH-deh ehl eh-lee-KOHP-teh-roh ah-teh-rree-SAHR ah-KEE

### The submarine has been used in war
*El submarino ha sido usado en la guerra*
Ehl soob-mah-REE-noh ah SEE-doh oo-SAH-doh ehn lah GEE-rrah

### That coach is quite old
*Ese carruaje es bastante viejo*
EH-seh Kah-rroo-AH-heh ehs bahs-TAHN-teh vee-EH-hoh

### Call a taxi
*Llama un taxi*
YAH-mah oon TAHK-see

### Stop there, please
*Para allí por favor*
PAH-rah ah-YEE pohr fah-VOHR

### Wait here
*Espera aquí*
Ehs-PEH-rah ah-KEE

### Can I transfer?
*¿Puedo hacer trasbordo?*
PWEH-doh ah-SEHR trahs-BOHR-doh

### You need to get off the bus now
*Tienes que bajarte del bus ahora*
Tee-EH-nehs keh bah-HAHR-teh dehl boos ah-OH-rah

### I am waiting in my car
*Estoy esperando en mi coche*
Ehs-TOH-ee ehs-peh-RAHN-doh ehn mee KOH-cheh

**A single ticket to…**
*Un billete de ida para…*
Oon bee-YEH-teh deh EE-dah PAH-rah

**A return ticket to**
*Un billete de ida y vuelta a…*
Oonv bee-YEH-teh deh voo-EHL-tah ah…

**Is everyone ready?**
*¿Está todo el mundo listo?*
Ehs-TAH TOH-doh ehl MOON-doh LEES-toh

**He plays tennis**
*Él juega tenis*
Ehl hoo-EH-gah TEH-nees

**We play basketball in the court**
*Jugamos al baloncesto en la cancha*
Hoo-GAH-mohs ahl bah-lohn-SEHS-toh ehn lah KAHN-chah

**They are having dancing lessons**
*Están teniendo clases de baile*
Ehs-THAN the-nee-EHN-doh KLAH-sehs deh bah-EE-leh

**We need a new bike for cycling**
*Necesitamos una bici nueva para hacer ciclismo*
Neh-seh-see-TAH-mohs OO-nah BEE-see noo-EH-vah PAH-rah ah-SEHR see-CLEES-moh

**Do you compete doing gymnastics?**
*¿Compites haciendo gimnasia?*
Kohm-PEE-tehs ah-see-EHN-doh heem-NAH-see-ah

**I would like to join the rowing team**
*Me gustaría unirme al equipo de remo*
Meh goos-tah-REE-ah oo-NEER-meh ahl eh-KEE-poh deh REH-moh

**We go skiing every winter**
*Vamos a esquiar todos los inviernos*
VAH-mohs ah ehs-kee-AHR TOH-dohs lohs een-vee-EHR-nohs

**Go surfing**
*Ve a hacer surf*
Veh ah ah-SEHR Soorf

**Have you ever practised jumping?**
*¿Alguna vez has practicado salto?*
Ahl-GOO-nah vehs ahs prahk-tee-KAH-doh SAHL-toh

**I like swimming**
*Me gusta la natación*
Meh GOOS-tah lah nah-tah-see-OHN

**How many players do you need in baseball?**
*¿Cuántos jugadores necesitas en béisbol?*
KWAHN-tohs hoo-gah-DOH-rehs neh-seh-SEE-tahs ehn BEH-ees-bohl

**Do you like soccer?**
*¿Te gusta el fútbol?*
The GOOS-tah ehl FOOT-bohl

**Chess is an underrated sport**
*El ajedrez es un deporte infravalorado*
Ehl ah-heh-DREHS ehs oon deh por TEH een-frah-vah-loh-RAH-doh

**She is a famous athlete**
*Ella es una athleta famosa*
EH-yah ehs OO-nah ahth-LEH-tah fah-MOH-sah

**I am a runner**
*Soy corredor*
SOH-ee koh-rreh-DOHR

**We practise boxing**
*Practicamos boxeo*
prahk-tee-KAH-mohs bok-SEH-oh

**I like horse-riding**
*Me gusta montar a caballo*
Meh GOOS-tah mohn-TAHR ah kah-BAH-yoh

**Did you go to that run?**
*¿Fuiste a esa carrera?*
Foo-EHS-teh ah EH-sah kah-RREH-rah

**Let's play this match**
*Vamos a jugar este partido*
VAH-mohs ah hoo-GAHR EHS-the pahr-TEE-doh

**This is a single player**
*Esto es para un solo jugador*
EHS-toh ehs PAH-rah oon SOH-loh hoo-gah-DOHR

**They passed to quarter finals**
*Pasaron a cuartos de final*
Pah-SAH-rohn ah koo-AHR-tohs deh fee-NAHL

**We did not get to semifinals**
*No llegamos a semifinales*
Noh yeh-GAH-mohs ah seh-mee-fee-NAH-lehs

**They made it into the finals**
*Llegaron a las finales*
Yeh-GAH-rohn ah lahs fee-NAH-lehs

**You are the winner**
*Eres es la ganadora (feminine)*
EH rehs lah gah-nah-DOH-rah

*Eres el ganador (masculine)*
EH rehs ehl gah-nah-DOHR

**We got second place**
*Quedamos segundos*
Keh-DAH-mohs seh-GOON-dohs

**We have the third place**
*Quedamos terceros*
Keh-DAH-mohs tehr SEH rohs

**You are a loser**
*Eres un perdedor*
EH-rehs oon pehr-deh-DOHR

**They are eliminated**
*Están eliminados*
ehs-TAHN eh-lee-mee-NAH-doh

**My team has been classified**
*Mi equipo ha sido clasificado*
Mee eh-KEE-poh ah SEE-doh klah-see-fee-KAH-doh

**You won the award**
*Ganaste el premio*
Gah-NAHS-teh ehl PREH-mee-oh

**They competed against us**
*Ellos han competido en contra nuestra*
EH-yohs ahn kohm-peh-TEE-doh ehn KOHN-trah h noo EHS trah

**Our team won**
*Nuestro equipo ha ganado*
Noo-EHS-troh eh-KEE-poh ah gah-NAH-doh

**The audience was cheering their team**
*La audiencia animaba su equipo*
Lah ah-oo-dee-EHN-see-ah ah-nee-MAH bah soo eh-KEE-poh

**When is the tournament?**
*¿Cuándo es el torneo?*
KWAHN-doh ehs ehl tohr-NEH-oh

**The competition has just finished**
*La competición acaba de finalizar*
Lah kohm-peh-tee-see-OHN ah-KAH-bah deh fee-nah-lee-SAHR

**He is the worst player**
*Él es el peor jugador*
Ehl ehs ehl peh-OHR joo-gah-DOHR

**This team has improved a lot**
*Este equipo ha mejorado mucho*
EHS-teh eh-KEE-poh ah meh-hoh-RAH-doh MOO-choh

**I support this team**
*Yo apoyo este equipo*
Yoh ah-POH-yoh EHS-teh eh-KEE-poh

**I love risky sports**
*Me encantan los deportes de riesgo*
Meh ehn-KAHN-tahn lohs deh-POHR-tehs deh ree-EHS-goh

**Bungee jumping is amazing**
*Hacer puenting es increíble*
Ah-SEHR poo-EHN-teeng ehs een-kreh-EE-bleh

**My children go to kindergarten**
*Mis hijos van a la guardería*
Mees EE-hohs vahn ah lah goo-ahr-deh-REE-ah

**We are starting school**
*Vamos a empezar el colegio*
VAH-mohs ah chm-peh-SAHR ehl koh-LEH-hee-oh

**I'llgo to college next month**
*Iré al instituto el mes que viene*
ee REH ahl eehns-tee-TOO-toh ehl mehs keh vee-EH-neh

**I haven't gone to the university**
*No he ido a la universidad*
Noh eh EE-doh ah lah oo-nee-vehr-see-DAHD

**My teacher inspires me**
*Mi maestro me inspira*
Mee mah-EHS-troh meh eens-PEE-rah

**That professor is very bad**
*Ese profesor es muy malo*
EH-seh pro-feh-SOHR ehs MOO-ee
MAH-loh

**He is my tutor**
*Es mi tutor*
Ehs mee too-TOHR

**Who is the principal?**
*¿Quién es el director?*
Kee-EHN ehs ehl dee-rehk-TOHR

**You need a diary for your home-
work**
*Necesitas una agenda para tus
deberes*
Neh-seh-SEE-tahs OO-nah ah-HEHN-
dah PAH-rah toos deh-BEH-rehs

**I study English**
*Yo estudio inglés*
Yoh ehs-TOO-dee-oh een-GLEHS

**I am bad at Maths**
*Soy malo en matemáticas*
SOH-ee MAH-loh ehn mah-teh-MAH-
tee-kahs

**What is the purpose of this
project?**
*¿Cuál es el propósito de este
proyecto?*
KWAHL ehs ehl proh-POH-see-toh deh
EHS-teh proh- YEHK-toh

**Technology is fun**
*La tecnología es divertida*
Lah Tehk-noh-loh-HEE-ah ehs dee-vehr-
TEE-dah

**Languages are very important
in education**
*Los idiomas son muy impor-
tantes en la educación*
Lohs ee-dee-OH-mahs sohn MOO-ee
eem-poohr-TAHN-tehs ehn lah eh-doo-
kah-see-OHN

**I like music**
*Me gusta la música*
Meh GOOS-tah lah MOO-see-kah

**They are young students**
*Son estudiantes jóvenes*
Sohn ehs-too-dee-AHN-tehs HOH-veh-
nehs

**Sciences are difficult**
*Las ciencias son difíciles*
Lahs see-EHN-see-ahs sohn dee-FEE-
see-lehs

**Do you have a degree?**
*¿Tienes una carrera?*
Tee-EH-nehs OO-nah kah-RREH-rah

**Where is my ruler?**
*¿Dónde está mi regla?*
DOHN-deh ehs-TAH mee REH-glah

**I lost my pencil**
*Perdí mi lápiz*
pehr-DEE mee LAH-pees

**Look at the board**
*Mira la pizarra*
MEE-rah lah pee-SAH-rrah

**It is break time**
*Es hora del recreo*
Ehs OH-rah dehl reh-KREH-oh

**Who is in the class group?**
*¿Quién está en el grupo de clase?*
Kee-EHN ehs-TAH ehn ehl GROO-poh
deh KLAH-seh

**I have homework to do**
*Tengo tarea que hacer*
TEHN-goh tah-REH-ah keh ah-SEHR

**It is easy**
*Es fácil*
Ehs FAH-seel

**It is difficult**
*Es difícil*
Ehs dee-FEE-seel

**Are you listening?**
*¿ Están escuchando?*
*Ehs-TAHN ehs-koo-CHAHN-doh*

**Yes, we are listening to you**
*Sí, te estamos escuchando*
See teh ehs-TAH-mohs ehs-koo-CHAHN-
doh

**I must study now**
*Debo estudiar ahora*
DEH-boh ehs-too-dee-AHR ah-OH-rah

**I will study harder**
*Estudiaré más*
Ehs-too-dee-ah-REH mahs

**Good luck in your exam**
*Buena suerte en tu examen*
Boo-EH-nah soo-EHR-teh ehn too ek-
SAH-mehn

**This is my classroom**
*Esta es mi clase*
EHS-tah ehs mee KLAH-seh

**I have studied during my w[ ]
life**
*He estudiado durante toda mi
vida*
Eh ehs-too-dee-AH-doh doo-RAHN-teh
TOH-dah mee VEE-dah

**I  paid for all my studies**
*Yo pagué todos mis estudios*
Yoh pah-GEH TOH-dohs mees ehs-
TOO-dee-ohs

**My friend graduated last year**
*Mi amigo se graduó el año pas-
ado*
Mee ah-MEE-goh seh grah-doo-OH ehl
AH-nyoh pah-SAH-doh

**I have failed many exams**
*He  perdido muchos exámenes*
Eh   pehr DIH doh MOO-chohs ehk-
SAH-meh-nehs

**He is the headteacher in this
high school**
*Él es el director de este insti-
tuto*
Ehl ehs ehl dee-REHK-tohr  deh EHS-teh
eens-tee-TOO-toh

**I have a doubt about it**
*Tengo una duda sobre esto*
TEHN-goh OO-nah DOO-dah SOH-
breh EHS-toh

**What are the topics for the next
assessment?**
*¿Cuáles son los temas para la
siguiente evaluación?*
KWAH-lehs sohn lohs TEH-mahs PAH-
rah lah see-gee-EHN-teh eh-vah-loo-ah-
see-OHN

## We need a dictionary
*Necesitamos un diccionario*
Neh-seh-see-TAH-mohs oon deek-see-oh-NAH-ree-oh

## I need to talk to the headteacher
*Necesito hablar con el director*
Neh-see-SEE-toh ah-BLAHR kohn ehl dee-rehk-TOHR

## My results have been awful
*Mis resultados han sido desas-trosos*
Mees reh-sool-TAH-dohs ahn SEE-doh deh-sahs-TROH-sohs

## This subject is difficult to understand
*Esta asignatura es difícil de entender*
EHS-tahs ah-seeg-nah-TOO-rah ehs dee-FEE-seel deh ehn-tehn-DEHR

## I will study one year abroad
*Estudiaré un año en el extranjero*
Ehs-too-dii-ah-REH oon AH-nyo ehn el ehks-trahn-HEH-roh

## Many people is studying my degree
*Muchas personas estudian mi carrera*
MOO-chahs pehr-SOH-nahs ehs-TOO-dee-ahn mee kah-RREH-rah

## I would like to have a job related to my degree
*Me gustaría tener un trabajo relacionado con mi carrera*
Meh goos-tah-REE-ah oon trah-BAH-hoh reh-lah-see-oh-NAH-doh kohn mee kah-RREH-rah

## The studies are important for the future
*Los estudios son importantes para el futuro*
Lohs ehs-TOO-dee-ohs sohn eem-pohr-TAHN-tehs PAH-rah ehl foo-TOO-roh

## I have several options for next year
*Tengo varias opciones para el año que viene*
TEHN-goh VAH-ree-ahs ohp-see-OH-ne-hs PAH-rah ehl AH-nyoh keh vee-EH-neh

## I would like to study languages
*Me gustaría aprender idiomas*
Meh goos-tah-REE-ah ah-prehn-DEHR ee-dee-OH-mahs

## The pupils are unhappy with the results
*Los alumnos están tristes con los resultados*
Lohs ah-LOOM-nohs ehs-TAHN TREES tehs kohn lohs reh-sool-TAH-dohs

## Tomorrow we have our final exams
*Mañana tenemos nuestros exámenes finales*
Mah-NYAH-nah teh-NEH-mohs noo EHS trohs ehk-SAH-meh-nehs fee-NAH-lehs

## You need high qualifications for your degree
*Necesitas notas altas para tu carrera*
Neh-seh-SEE-tahs NOH-tahs AHL-tahs PAH-rah too kah-RREH-rah

### I have lost my papers
*Perdí mis papeles*
pehr-DEE- mees pah-PEH-lehs

### She was cheating in the exam
*Ella estaba copiando en el examen*
EH-yah ehs-TAH-bah koh-pee-AHN-doh ehn ehl ek-SAH-mehn

### Tomorrow we have a trip
*Mañana tenemos una excursión*
Mah-NYAH-nah teh-NEH-mohs OO-nah ehks-koor-see-OHN

### This guy was expelled of his university
*Este chico fue expulsado de su universidad*
EHS-teh CHEE-koh foo-EH ehks-pool-SAH-doh deh soo oo-nee-vehr-see-DAHD

### I am sorry but we have to call your parents
*Lo siento, pero tenemos que llamar a tus padres*
Loh see-EHN-toh PEH-roh teh-NEH-mohs keh yah-MAHR ah toos PAH-drehs

# Numbers

**Zero**
*Cero*
CEH-roh

**One**
*Uno*
OO-noh

**Two**
*Dos*
Dohs

**Three**
*Tres*
Trehs

**Four**
*Cuatro*
KWAH-tro

**Five**
*Cinco*
SEEN-koh

**Six**
*Seis*
SEH-ees

**Seven**
*Siete*
See-EH-teh

**Eight**
*Ocho*
OH-choh

**Nine**
*Nueve*
Noo-EH-veh

**Ten**
*Diez*
*Dee-EHS*

**Eleven**
*Once*
OHN-seh

**Twelve**
*Doce*
DOH-seh

**Thirteen**
*Trece*
TREH-seh

**Fourteen**
*Catorce*
Cah-TOHR-seh

**Fifteen**
*Quince*
KEEN-seh

**Sixteen**
*Dieciseis*
Dee-eh-see-SEH-ees

**Seventeen**
*Diecisiete*
Dee-eh-see-see-EH-teh

**Eighteen**
*Dieciocho*
Dee-eh-see-OH-choh

**Nineteen**
*Diecinueve*
Dee-eh-see-noo-EH-veh

**Twenty**
*Veinte*
Veh-EEN-teh

**Twenty-one**
*Veintiuno*
Veh-een-tee-OO-noh

**Twenty-two**
*Veintidós*
Veh-een-tee-DOHS

**Twenty-three**
*Veintitrés*
Veh-een-tee-TREHS

**Twenty-four**
*Veinticuatro*
Veh-een-tee-KWAH-troh

**Twenty-five**
*Veinticinco*
Veh-een-tee-SEEN-koh

**Twenty-six**
*Veintiseis*
Veh-een-tee-SEH-ees

**Twenty-seven**
*Veintisiete*
Veh-een-tee-see-EH-teh

**Twenty-eight**
*Veintiocho*
Veh-een-tee-OH-choh

**Twenty-nine**
*Veintinueve*
Veh-een-tee-noo-EH-veh

**Thirty**
*Treinta*
Treh-EEN-tah

**Forty**
*Cuarenta*
Kwah-REHN-tah

**Fifty**
*Cincuenta*
Seen-KWEHN-tah

**Sixty**
*Sesenta*
Seh-SEHN-tah

**Seventy**
*Setenta*
Seh-TEHN-tah

**Eighty**
*Ochenta*
Oh-CHEHN-tah

**Ninety**
*Noventa*
Noh-VEHN-tah

**One-hundred**
*Cien*
See-EHN

**Two-hundred**
*Doscientos*
Dohs-see-EHN-tohs

**Five-hundred**
*Quinientos*
Kee-nee-EHN-tohs

**One-thousand**
*Mil*
Meel

**One-hundred-thousand**
*Cien mil*
See-ehn-MEEL

**One million**
*Un millón*
Oon mee-YOHN

**One billion**
*Un billón*
Oon bee-YOHN

# Date & Time

**My favourite season is spring**
*Mi estación favorita es la primavera*
Mee ehs-tah-see-OHN fah-voh-REE-tah ehs lah pree-mah-VEH-rah

**I will visit you in summer**
*Te voy a visitar en verano*
Teh VOH-ee ah vee-see-TAHR ehn veh-RAH-noh

**I like taking pictures in autumn**
*Me gusta tomar fotos en otoño*
Meh GOOS-tah toh-MAHR FOH-tohs ehn oh-TOH-nyoh

**It is very late**
*Es muy tarde*
Ehs MOO-ee TAHR-deh

**Where are you going in winter?**
*¿A dónde vas en invierno?*
Ah DOHN-deh vahs ehn een-vee-EHR-noh

**Time has gone so fast**
*El tiempo ha pasado tan rápido*
Ehl tee-EHM-poh ah pah-SAH-doh TAHN RAH-pee-doh

**It is too early**
*Es demasiado temprano*
Ehs deh-mah-see-AH-doh tehm-PRAH-noh

**It is nighttime here**
*Aquí es de noche*
Ah-KEE ehs deh NOH-cheh

**It is daylight here**
*Aquí es de día*
Ah-KEE ehs deh DEE-ah

**January**
*Enero*
Eh-NEH-roh

**February**
*Febrero*
Feh-BREH-roh

**March**
*Marzo*
MAHR-soh

**April**
*Abril*
Ah-BREEL

**May**
*Mayo*
MAH-yoh

**June**
*Junio*
HOO-nee-oh

**July**
*Julio*
HOO-lee-oh

**August**
*Agosto*
Ah-GOHS-toh

**September**
*Septiembre*
Sehp-tee-EHM-breh

**October**
*Octubre*
Ohk-TOO-breh

**November**
*Noviembre*
Noh-vee-EHM-breh

**December**
*Diciembre*
Dee-see-EHM-breh

**Monday**
*Lunes*
LOO-nehs

**Tuesday**
*Martes*
MAHR-tehs

**Wednesday**
*Miércoles*
Mee-EHR-koh-lehs

**Thursday**
*Jueves*
Hoo-EH-vehs

**Friday**
*Viernes*
Vee-EHR-nehs

**Saturday**
*Sábado*
SAH-bah-doh

**Sunday**
*Domingo*
Doh-MEEN-goh

**It's ... o'clock**
*Son las ... en punto*
Sohn lahs .... ehn POON-toh

**It's half past...**
*Son las ... y media*
Sohn lahs .... ee NEH-dee-ah

**It's quarter past…**
*Son las … y cuarto*
Sohn lahs … ee koo-AHR-toh

**It's quarter to…**
*Son las … menos cuarto*
Sohn lahs … MEH-nohs koo-AHR-toh

**It's ten past …**
*Son las … y diez*
Sohn lahs … ee dee-EHS

**It's five past …**
*Son las … y cinco*
Sohn lahs … ee SEEN-KOH

**It's twenty past …**
*Son las … y veinte*
Sohn lahs … ee VEH-EEN-TEH

**It's five to…**
*Son las … menos cinco*
Sohn lahs … MEH-nohs SEEN-koh

**It's twenty-five to…**
*Son las … menos veinticinco*
Sohn lahs … MEH-nohs veh-een-tee-SEEN-koh

**It's ten to…**
*Son las … menos diez*
Sohn lahs … MEH-nohs dee-EHS

**Day**
*Día*
DEE-ah

**Afternoon**
*Tarde*
TAHR-deh

**Night**
*Noche*
NOH-cheh

**What is today's date?**
*¿ Qué fecha e es hoy?*
KEH FEH-chah ehs OH-ee

**What is the time?**
*¿Qué hora es?*
Keh OH-rah ehs

**When is the next holiday?**
*¿Cuándo son las próximas vacaciones?*
KWAHN-doh sohn lahs PROHK-see-mahs vah-kah-see-OH-nehs

**What time does the store open?**
*¿A qué hora abre la tienda?*
Ah keh OH-rah AH breh lah tee-EHN-dah

**What time are we meeting at?**
*¿A qué hora hemos quedado?*
Ah keh OH-rah EH-mohs keh-DAH-doh

**What time do you wake up?**
*¿A qué hora te despiertas?*
Ah keh OH-rah teh dehs-pee-EHR-tahs

**Do you have a watch?**
*¿Tienes un reloj?*
Tee-EH-nehs oon reh-LOH

**The calendar is from this month**
*El calendario es de este mes*
Ehl kah-lehn-DAH-ree-oh ehs deh EHS-the mehs

**When is sunset?**
*¿Cuándo es la puesta de sol?*
KWAHN-doh ehs lah poo-EHS-tah deh sohl

**When is sunrise?**
*¿Cuándo es el amanecer?*
KWAHN-doh ehs ehl ah-mah-neh-SEHR

**I am leaving now**
*Me voy*
Meh VOH-ee

**It is time for dinner**
*Es hora de cenar*
Ehs OH-rah deh seh-NAHR

**I will do it tomorrow**
*Lo haré mañana* Loh ah-REH ma-NYAH-nah

**I wake up late**
*Me despierto tarde*
Meh dehs-pee-EHR-toh TAHR-deh

**I wake up early**
*Me despierto temprano*
Meh dehs-pee-EHR-toh tehm-PRAH-noh

**I came the day before**
*Yo vine el día antes*
Yoh VEE-neh ehl DEE-ah AHN-tehs

# Conclusion

**C**ongratulations! You have reached the end of the book and officially learned over 2000 ways to express yourself in Spanish!

Give yourself a pat on the back, because you are one step closer to reaching fluency .
Even though you have unlocked a huge amount of incredibly useful day-to-day phrases the learning should not end there.

Keeping this book by your side and revisiting it's material will be the best way to internalize them and use them in the correct situation. Context is crucial, as well as reinforcing your knowledge with other diverse Spanish materials. Here are a few quick tips so you can make the most of your Spanish Phrasebook and expand your vocabulary even further:

## 1. Practice for 30 minutes every day:

**C**onsistent practice is far better than batching hours of study and practice all in one go. This is because consistency is the only way things stick in your long term memory. Make sure to constantly pick up the book and read the words, saying them out loud and taking note of your mistakes so you can correct them along the way.

## 2. Read while listening to the Audiobook:

**A** very effective way of learning a new language is by using the RwL (reading while listening) method.

Studies have proven that this method can boost verbal fluency, help you with correct pronunciation and also internalize grammar rules. Be sure to grab the audiobook version of this book – it will literally triple your learning speed!

### 3. Study with a partner or in groups:

It's always best to go on an adventure with others – even if it's a language learning adventure! Not only will you enjoy yourself more, but the added factor of accountability will force you to learn even quicker.
Look to the Internet for support in various reddit forums and Facebook groups and websites like iTalki that offer paid services to accelerate to fluency. You'll be surprised to find thousands going through the same experiences as you!

Make sure you check out our other "Spanish for Beginners" book and good luck on your journey to fluency.

### Hasta el fuego!

### Fluency Faster

Made in the USA
Las Vegas, NV
15 July 2021

26505755R00069